Investing by Spread Bettir

Spread B
for Losers

Part 1: How to break even

John Austin, Ph.D.

Investing by Spread Betting, by John Austin

Published by Enigma Scientific Publications

First published in England in 2015 by Enigma Scientific Publications, Berkshire, UK
http://www.enigmascientific.co.uk

First print version 12 September, 2015.
Createspace edition 16 September, 2015.
ISBN number 9781517364090

Contents

1.Introduction

The majority of private investors who try financially leveraged products lose money. I understand your pain because I've already lost a packet over the years. I refer of course to products such as spread betting, and options trading. I have tried all these methods in the past, but had no overall success. What has now changed is that I have put in the time and effort to understand how to trade more sensibly and the situation has turned around. I believe that anyone who puts in the time and effort can succeed and make a profit but we must learn to walk before we can run. The first step is to break even and this book is a short summary of my conclusions and personal experience over the last 6 months. Part 2 will, I hope, see the transition towards significant profits by applying the principles of the material here.

Financially leveraged products include spread betting. In the USA (and presumably other countries as well) similar products exist, e.g. options (although they have a different risk profile) and the e-mini Dow offered by the Chicago Board of Trade. The point is that the same basic principles apply to everything, so I will concentrate on spread betting, with one short chapter on options. With financially leveraged products, you put up a small deposit, say 0.5% and then if the market moves just a small amount you can make or lose a disproportionate amount of your deposit. This is not dissimilar in principle to house purchase. In that case you might take out a 90% mortgage and put 10% down as a deposit. For example, suppose you buy a house for £300k, with a £30k deposit. You pay the mortgage for a year and if you're lucky the house price goes up 10%. The house is now worth £330k but your mortgage is still £270k so you now have £60k equity and your equity has doubled. Spread betting is similar in principle: the company you spread bet with effectively lends you the 99.5% cost of the market and off you go. However, they are a bit like loan sharks: if your equity drops, they want their money back, pronto! In the case of the house purchase a drop in the house price, say to £250k would leave you £20k negative equity, but as long as you can pay the mortgage, your mortgage company will leave you in peace. Options are a half way house: you get some of the advantages of spread betting, and you can never lose more than your purchase price. However, the returns are lower, and the market spread is higher.

Spread betting by contrast can be hazardous to your health! It is easy to lose a lot of money very quickly, and then you will be scrabbling around for funds to restore your equity (and sanity). That is one of the reasons I lost money in the past and I think by adopting a number of measures you can avoid this situation. Whether or not you can make significant money this way depends on a variety of factors. I generally have a dogged determination and despite my significant losses in the past, I have again started to apply my previous scientific training to the task at hand to understand market trading better. Bear in mind that the average account holder trades for about 6 months[1], although that figure is perhaps a bit apocryphal. Most spread bettors give up, presumably because their losses are too large but you don't usually hear from the losers. It's embarrassing to let people know you've lost money, especially when it's supposed to be so easy! Somehow, losing money questions your manhood (and it is mostly men who have the appetite for this sort of risk). But of course this is nonsense.

So, I have no illusions over spread betting, and you should not either: spread betting is difficult and time consuming, despite comments from "get rich quick" charlatans. My illusion if you like (or call it arrogance!) is that there is nothing I can't

Investing by Spread Betting, by John Austin

understand if I put my mind to it: the benefits of a Cambridge PhD, I'm afraid! The point is that financial trading is about seeking patterns and relationships, and separating signals from the noise. These are exactly the techniques that scientific research demands. But, despite my 30 year research career, although I have been able to make money with regular share trading, I have previously been unsuccessful with leveraged products, probably because I have not applied myself properly. This book, then, although containing the basic material needed for success is mainly a personal account of my experiences during the learning process.

In Chapter 2, I summarise the basics of spread betting and in Chapter 3 describe analysis tools which help to trade the market more intelligently. Chapter 4 provides guidance on what markets to trade and the best times of day for doing so. In stock market lore there are a number of sayings that supposedly help to trade the markets and I describe these in Chapter 5. In practice they are bordering on the meaningless, as we shall see, but it is worth having some sort of mantra to work with, even if you break your own rules from time to time. I expect you have read stock market reports which "explain" why the market has gone up or down. Again, this is often quite meaningless, but with a mantra you can at least give yourself some peace of mind. Chapter 6 briefly describes options trading, comparing and contrasting with spread betting. Chapter 7 forms a collection of the trades that I have made with financial spread betting so that you can see it for what it is: warts and all. Chapter 8 concludes by summarising the material. Like the clichés of Chapter 5, a lot of this is somewhat subjective. Alas, this is not rocket science. If it were, money making would be predictable and a lot easier!

Investing by Spread Betting, by John Austin

2. Spread Betting Basics

2.1 Getting started

(i) Identify a spread betting company

The first step is to identify a spread betting company to work with, for example as summarised here[2]. The information given there may be a little out of date, and I would suggest that you contact the firms for their current charges before deciding who to work with. I've chosen IG markets, but others such as Corespreads and DF Markets may be just as good. I've known IG from a long time ago, so I'm comfortable with them. They also now have my ISA account, so it's convenient to have both investments under the same roof. Certainly IG (and I expect other companies as well) enable money to be transferred very easily from a bank account. They are very thorough in asking what your income is: it's a bit disconcerting that already they seem to be planning on you losing and needing regular infusions of cash into your account!

(ii) Operate a demonstration account

Initially you should run a demo account. IG only allow a non-customer to run a demo account for a few weeks and then to continue you need to start again with real money. For me, two weeks wasn't long enough to test my proposed trading strategy. With a demo account, you have a nominal £10k virtual money and off you go. However, it is not real money and so you may be more liable to take extra risks than if it were your own. Personally, I don't like to be parted from my cash, so a real account can be very different! I think just operating a demo account is entertaining and could be sold as a computer game, if it isn't already.

(iii) Learn the ropes

The spread betting company will have a lot of information explaining the basics and providing education and information to help you trade better. It is in the interests of the company that you make profits as this encourages more trades and makes more money for them. Also, they don't have to recruit your replacement. During my first three months of trading, I made no money for myself and perhaps £1000 in spreads for the company: not a very good deal! So, I was basically working like an apprentice for no salary. This couldn't go on!

(iv) Equipment

You probably already have the necessary equipment to trade. Spread betting companies will offer charts and up to the second prices with which you can make decisions. You need to supply a computer with a decent internet connection. Even a mobile phone might in principle substitute the computer, but I'm old school, I suppose, and I need a decent size screen to nuance the details. My mother is even older school and doesn't even have an internet service! So, when I spend short breaks with her, I carry my (40 cm) laptop and bring an internet dongle, which connects into one of my USB ports. On a per Gbyte basis, they are quite expensive to access the internet, which they do by the mobile phone network. I have a pay as you go Vodafone dongle, which costs £10 for just one Gbyte of data. Trading and the checking of emails needs about 100 Mbytes per day, so the dongle would last about 10 days. Obviously it's well worth buying as it can pay for itself in 5 minutes.

I haven't found train internet services reliable enough for trading. There is nothing like the sudden loss of internet signal to create panic in your mind! On the other hand, trading while you're on the train can be effective with the dongle. In a recent journey back from Plymouth to Reading, I fired up my laptop at about 4 pm, just as we were leaving Plymouth, and made a quick trade, picking up £14. Although it is easy to get addicted to trading, due to the adrenaline rush as you make the trade, I like to sit back and take it easy when I'm on the train! Nonetheless, it was useful for me to have tried the experiment because I can then perhaps repeat the exercise when closing a running position might be more critical.

(v) Taxes

I have good news, sort of! Under current UK law, gains from spread betting are tax free[3]. You might think this is remarkably generous of the government, but they are not stupid! Well, the senior civil servants aren't anyway. The point is that tax regulations are symmetric: you can claim a loss in one place against a gain in another place. If spread betting gains were taxed, then the spread betting losses incurred by the majority of people would counteract their gains elsewhere and reduce their overall tax burden. So, paradoxically, the government can increase its tax take by making spread betting tax free. To do this, it pretends that the process is gambling as opposed to "investing". But I assure you, dear reader, I don't gamble, not even on the national lottery! However, if you were to be successful enough to trade for a living, the profits could be considered as an income and might be taxable. Heads I win, tails you lose, says the Inland Revenue!

The USA is different. Of course nobody fills in their own tax form there, they are just totally incomprehensible. So everybody uses either an accountant or you buy software for $40 or something and do it on your computer. So I don't really know the rules. However, one particular year, 6 months after having completed my tax form, I received a demand for £25k in overdue taxes. This was a bit frightening, bear in mind that my salary at the time was only about $110k. It turned out that the company I had used to trade leveraged products informed the Inland Revenue of my $75k in options and contract *sales* so I received a tax bill as if the entire sales were all profit. It never occurred to anyone that it might have cost something to buy those options and contracts in the first place. I just thought it was bizarre that the financial companies were apparently legally required to report my *sales* but not my *profits*. It required an enormous effort for me to go through hundreds of transactions to obtain the purchase price of all the options and to have to itemize (note the subtle use of the z there) each of them for the IR. We conclude from this that these leveraged products are treated as normal capital gains and taxed accordingly, but I wonder what happens in the country as a whole. Do people in the US lose money trading options, or are they better at it than Brits? Perhaps the US government doesn't mind reducing its tax intake slightly.

2.2 Running Your Account

(i) Jargon

Once you have an account, even just a demo account you will be ready to learn the jargon of spread betting. This seems strange at first, but it is easy enough once you get the hang of it. Trades are buys or sells in pounds per point. Note that you can go long (buy) or short (sell without first owning) a stock. This is always a great bargaining point for spread betting "you can make money on the way up and you can make money on the way down", which sounds wonderful until you realise the corollary: "you can lose money on the way up and lose money on the way down"! Going short sounds a bit strange at first, but if you think about it logically, a stock market transaction consists of a buy and a sell, so why should it matter what order you do them in? There are technical issues regarding selling the more obscure stock, but I would suggest that you steer clear of them anyway, at least until you know what you're doing. Once you have bought or sold you have a position "open". It remains "open" until you do the opposite action -- sell if previously bought or buy if previously sold. The position is then "closed" and you can go away and have a soothing cup of tea!

Investing by Spread Betting, by John Austin

You will probably need something soothing, even if you've made a profit, as if you trade on short timescales, the adrenaline would have been pumping through your system.

If you've bought a stock at £1 per point then for every point that the stock moves up, you gain £1, while for every point that the stock moves down you lose £1. For individual stocks, one point is 1p while for indices 1 point is 1 index point. You can also trade currencies in the same way as stocks on a pounds per point basis. For example, for the £/$ exchange rate, 1 point is 0.01 c.

Stocks are easy to understand as £1 per point is equivalent to buying or selling 100 shares. Indices are also easy to understand: IG markets has a minimum of £2 per point on the FTSE so when you buy, you are effectively buying £14000 of stock if the FTSE is at 7000. The deposit, or in the jargon "margin", needed in your account is £70. During especially volatile times, this margin may be increased by the company, although IG usually give advance warning. The physical meaning of exchange rates is a bit more difficult. For example buying £1 per point on the £/$ rate means that you are selling $ or buying pounds. For example, if the exchange rate is $1.50 per pound, the quoted price would be 15000 and £1 per point means that your selling £15000 of dollars. It's a bit odd, as the equivalent capital changes as the exchange rate changes, but it's best not to think about it. You can for example go long at 15000 at £1 per point and ignore the fact that you are trading currency, it could be anything. The main point is to watch the exchange rate or profit and if it reaches your target or stop, close the position and your cash account will be credited or debited accordingly.

As in the case of physical share and currency transactions, there is a difference between the buying and selling rates, and this difference, called the spread, is where spread betting gets its name. When you first trade, the position immediately goes to a loss, the amount of the spread. If you're skilful enough, this will quickly disappear and your position will move into profit. The company you work with makes its money from the spread, giving you the services you need to trade. Unlike you, it always makes money from every trade, so it's a bit like a casino operator! You take the risk, the company makes a charge against you. Of course if you make a profitable trade you get the money, but where does this come from?

There are two ways the company can do this. The first is that for common stocks and indices it can pair people off against each other. For example, I might be short and you might be long, so assuming we close our positions together I pay you for your profit, or the other way around. This can work for common stocks and indices. In this case the company usually has a large enough number of clients and by the statistics of large numbers, on average they don't know what they are doing! So they cancel out. If traders show a particular preference (long or short) then the company can buy or sell in the market. For example, if on average its clients are 75% long and 25% short, it needs to cover the 50% that are net long. To do this it simply buys in the market, regardless of the circumstances. It doesn't need to make any investment decision. That way if the longs close their positions, the company sells its stock to compensate. The company makes a profit on the stock sale, most of which it passes to the client. In rapidly moving markets or low liquidity (relatively few people playing, e.g. at night), the market spread will go up so that the company can cover potential losses.

(ii) Practicalities

I like to trade on short timescales – less than an hour or occasionally up to a few days. This often requires rapid execution of trades and one of the easiest way of doing this is to have a chart on your computer screen of the stock or commodity that you want to trade. IG markets, and I expect other companies as well, have a button that you can click on to open the trade. You first have to set the amount (£/pt) which I often do long before I open the trade itself. Then when you think conditions are right you can click on the appropriate button and execute the trade within a fraction of a second. The trade is executed at the appropriate time and then a small icon appears on the chart showing your running profit. The appearance of the icon often takes a second or two and in markets with a small spread, such as the FTSE, by the time the running profit or loss are displayed, you might even have a positive number! That is, the market may have already moved in your direction a distance greater than the spread. When this happens, it always makes me feel that little bit happier! You can close the position by clicking on the appropriate part of the icon. This gives the facility for very rapid trading. Obviously this isn't as good as the extremely rapid microsecond trading by professionals, but it is good enough for many purposes, for plebs like you and me!

(iii) Stops and Limits

Once you have your position up and running, you can set a stop loss (a point at which you close the position to limit further losses) or a limit (the price at which you close the position to crystalise a gain). I have used these sparingly, but many people swear by them [e.g, 4]. Personally, I think the jury is out. In the past I have set a stop loss, which is triggered, only to find the stock price reverses. So don't forget, a stop loss usually entails that you will guarantee losing money on the trade. Do you want that, or are you prepared to risk more for the sake of the market potentially reversing? This is always the dilemma, and there is no answer. Of course you can set your stop loss far from the stock price that it is very unlikely to be triggered, unless the sky is falling! In this case, is the stop loss doing anything at all? I accept that for trading in small stocks, some stop loss might be advisable, but I think these are too risky anyway and for these, the best strategy could be share ownership rather than spread betting.

There are less-advertised problems with stop losses. For individual stocks, it is not unusual for sudden spikes to occur in the price. These are major movements of the stock price perhaps of the order of 1% (smaller for indices and currencies) which only last for a few seconds. It has been suggested that market makers are not always entirely scrupulous during quiet market conditions. When spikes in the stock price occur, positions with a limit close to the current price can get closed, "stopped out" in the jargon. If you are a victim of price spikes, genuine or otherwise it is most irritating and has caused many a complaint to spread betting companies. In a similar vein, common indices, FTSE100, Dow etc., can become volatile in the pre or post market. For example you can trade the FTSE100 24 hours/day except for a short time over the weekend. Obviously the volume of trades is somewhat lower than during the day, but this off-market can generate unrealistic price swings. Of course the savvy investor can take advantage of these price swings, so it's not all doom and gloom, it's just that there is increased danger of stops being hit during the "off-market", the unofficial market outside opening hours. Of course you can avoid stops being hit by accident by not setting them in the first place!

A happy situation can occur if you are trading over several days, and the market price moves in your favour. You can then adjust the stop loss so that in fact you guarantee a profit even if your profit would then be more modest than the current level. For example, suppose that you have gone long of the FTSE at 6700 and it has moved to 6750. Then in principle you could set the stop loss at 6725 which would guarantee a 25 pt gain. At £2/pt this is not as much as the £100 you could have gained, but it's better than a kick in the pants. It's still a stop loss, though, and your choice could still have sacrificed £50 of profit. Over time, of course you can steadily nudge up your stop loss and then perhaps you will exit at a significant fraction of your peak profit. Personally, I'm usually too impatient for this, and when I see a good profit according to the circumstances, I generally close.

A limit represents the point at which you close your position for a profit. In the end it suffers from the same issues as the stop loss. I have in the past set a limit and the price has continued to soar well beyond the limit. If you set a limit, the position closes and you may lose potential profits. It is all a matter of perceived risk, and if your unable to watch the markets, e.g. it is time for bed, then setting a limit or stop can be useful. On the whole, though, if you trade less volatile products such as the FTSE, S&P500 or exchange rates then stop losses and limits may only be needed sparingly. Your spread betting company will likely (over)encourage you to use stop losses. Another issue to consider is that the indices and major stocks participate in the off-market. So if you trade a stock such as BT, you could find it marked down in price from the close of one day to the open of the next. Not only would you not have had the opportunity of trading off-market alongside the major indices, you could find that your stop has been hit at an unfavourable price as soon as the market opens. There are ways of avoiding this, e.g., with a guaranteed stop loss, but that costs extra.

2.3 An Investment Strategy

Before trading in earnest, you will need an investment strategy. If you go in blind, without any strategy, you are sure to lose most of your capital.

Your approach will depend in part on your appetite for risk. If you are prepared to take large risks then you need to be prepared for your positions to go significantly into the red at times before (hopefully) you make a profit. That then introduces the challenge: at which point do you pull the plug if the loss is large, or do you hang on for dear life hoping things will turn around? With a low risk strategy, you close a position when the loss has exceeded a certain amount, possibly using a stop loss, but this can be most frustrating if you close a position at a loss only to see the market turn around, which would have left you in profit if only you had hung on. The next time this happens, you might be tempted to allow bigger losses, but the same thing could happen again, and before long you have ratcheted up your risk profile until you are now relatively high risk as before. As in all investment ideas, there is no right or wrong answer, but all strategies involve some element of risk.

Investing by Spread Betting, by John Austin

Coupled to the idea of investment strategy is deciding what to trade. This is discussed in more detail in Chapter 4. Some markets are inherently less risky than others. For example, you could combine a high risk strategy (e.g. wide stops) with a low risk market (e.g. indices like the FTSE100 or Dow). The choice you make will depend on your knowledge of particular markets, your appetite for risk and simply what works well for you. Exploring all these issue may well take you 3 or more months of intensive trading before you have a clear strategy in place. One plausible strategy for example is to go long of the Dow or FTSE with no stops or limits and ignore the consequences for a year. This seems attractive because in most years the Dow or FTSE go up. The problem is that each of these indices can oscillate quite wildly and if your account is showing a £500 deficit, do you have the peace of mind to hold on for the good times? The temptation is to close your position at a significant loss, or even gain, and then the strategy has been changed. So the idea is to have a consistent strategy, but the same strategy may not be effective all the time, and your account may tread water, or even go down significantly during extended periods of time. There is of course no harm in changing your strategy at various times to suit changing market conditions. That obviously requires practice in the market.

While this book is primarily concerned with spread betting an alternative way of reducing risk is using options, and you could have a strategy of short term spread betting combined with longer term options trading. However, it is probably best to keep things simple initially and only combine options with spread betting once you already have a viable strategy with one or the other. Chapter 4 suggests some advantages and disadvantages of different markets while Chapter 6 describes options trading.

It is often suggested that you have multiple trades running in markets that are uncorrelated[5], or even anti-correlated. In other words, if one goes up, the other goes down. This has the advantage of reducing the volatility in the portfolio value, but not necessarily its long term gain. This would tend to require longer-term trades than I generally work with. The problem with multiple trades running for short time scales is that it requires a lot of concentration to keep track of what's happening. Stocks are often correlated, so you often need to branch out into commodities. For example gold and bond values generally go up as the stock market goes down. So a plausible strategy would be to be long of both bonds and stocks. Then if the bond price makes money, the stock market probably won't and the converse. This tends to reduce overall losses, but the corollary is that overall profits will be reduced as well. The point of spread betting in the first place is to use a leveraged product to make money. Rather than having anticorrelated trades, it seems to me to be better attuned to the movements of your chosen market and then just to trade that, be it gold, or the FTSE. You can increase the size of the trade to be consistent with your risk appetite. Of course supertraders may be long of the FTSE and short of gold at the same time, thereby increasing profits. But you and I are not supertraders, at least not yet!

2.4 Funding Your Account

IG markets (and I expect others as well) make it very easy to transfer money within minutes from a bank account to your spread betting account. It only takes seconds if everything is already set up. This is one thing that has changed: a decade or so ago, it used to take several days to get money from my bank account.

Whatever you do, make sure you have plenty of capital in your account. If a position goes against you, then you don't have to close and you can wait for the good times that may follow! The temptation is to use most of your capital for margin. This seems logical, as it makes the most use of your money and you can get a "bigger bang for your buck". The problem is that a lot of markets are correlated. In other words, if you go long of a number of different shares, then if the market tanks, it will probably bring everything down. Then you may find yourself scrabbling for margin and it is undignified to receive a phone call from your company asking for more money! That happened to me a few times when I first tried spread betting many years ago. Often, my other assets were elsewhere (or nonexistent) and I was obliged to close my positions only to see the shares recover later. That is how you are easily separated from your hard earned! Many years ago, also, it took days to get money transferred so there was often an embarrassing period between a call for more money, and actually being able to provide it. It's a bit like having the landlord coming around demanding the rent! Not that I have ever had to worry about that.

These days, I keep a modest amount of cash in my spread betting account, £1-2k, and typically trade the FTSE at £2/pt. Moreover my account has the psychologically important £1000+ in cash, significantly larger than potential losses on each trade (up to about £100) and significantly larger than the margin of only £67 or so for FTSE trading. So, I don't need to have to worry about margin. In the last 6 months I have made a small profit, but I am still learning. I expect within a year to be able to generate a more worthwhile profit.

3. Technical Analysis Basics

3.1 Introduction

Technical analysis is the nearest there is to the application of science to share prices. You start with a wiggly line (the share, index or commodity price as a function of time). Your mission (should you choose to accept it!) is to predict how that price will change in the future. The time dependent price for the past contains a signal, how the price is moving overall together with some "noise", which comes from random trades at different times. As you go to shorter time scales, it is more difficult to identify the signal and hence how the price will move a few minutes away, say. As you go to longer time scales, overall movements are larger but in some ways less predictable as sudden news can trigger changes.

The problem is not dissimilar to a number of problems in science. For example, 50 years or more ago, weather forecasting consisted largely of collecting observations and *extrapolating* them into the future. By extrapolating is meant the continuation of past trends into the future. This doesn't really work very well, so weather forecasting has moved on. The reason is that it doesn't allow for development. In other words, forecasters need to know whether a particular minor disturbance is going to develop into the next hurricane. Now, scientists use the physics of the atmosphere to provide predictions of how changes will occur. The physics is largely understood, although the representation of small, unobserved scales is a particular difficulty. As the physics can be really well described, a strategy is simply to solve the equations, and the next hurricane will then pop out of the solution. Solving these equations, though, is extremely demanding, requiring the world's fastest computers.

The stock market is different in that there is no set of physical equations to solve. Instead we are left with the extrapolation method, although modern methods are somewhat more sophisticated than that. Nonetheless, this works to a large extent because the markets have a psychology which is largely reproducible.

As you might guess, in common with most inexperienced traders, I used to ignore technical analysis, thinking that I knew better than market psychology. That's one reason why I lost money. So, dear reader, you cannot ignore technical analysis, if you are trading on timescales of a few days or less. The longer the timescale, the less important it is. But remember, the analysis is *post facto.* In other words, if something happens to affect the market, the technical analysis responds primarily to the prices, not the other way around. It is tempting to see a certain pattern in the charts and then to predict the share price from that, but this requires caution. The predictions often come true. This is for several reasons. First, technical analysis recognises patterns which reflect the extrapolation process. The second point is that the big boys know the rules. So technical analysis tends to become a self-fulfilling prophecy. This creates waves in the market prices, and you can make money by riding those waves. The biggest difficulty, though, is to force yourself to do what you should do. You may know that the extrapolation says one thing, but if you're sitting on a large loss or gain, you may be tempted to close the position for the gain to be crystalised or ride the losing position much longer than you should do.

This is where automatic trading systems can be effective[6]. Some systems can carry out the trade on your account, while other systems send a message to you, and you need to execute the trade manually. Both systems can do the mathematical extrapolation better than you or I and make the trade when opportunities are favourable. Such systems then close the trade at the right time. By contrast I know I get into a trade too early and close my profitable positions too early. If you know your weaknesses it helps with your trading, as you can perhaps modify your behaviour over time. However, if you can still make a reasonable amount of money then it may simply be better (lower stress levels) to accept your weaknesses and accept that you won't get the most from each trade. I have not used an actual automatic trading system which does the trade for me, but in the past I have subscribed to index advice services. Unfortunately, I did not make money possibly for two reasons: faced with a loss I often got out too early. Likewise I may have wanted to close winning positions early to ensure at least some profit. Another factor in advice services is that information is time critical. A particular advice service may indicate that you should buy the Dow at 17500, but in the 2 minutes that the buy recommendation gets to you, the market could have moved up 50 points, reducing your profit by this amount. Similarly, you never get the advertised performance on the closures of positions, so you get reduced performance at both buy and sell. I think, then that the best strategy is to understand the technical analysis yourself and then to trade accordingly. Even if I get in or out too early, at least I know the mistake I'm making, whereas with automatic systems you never really know why the trade has been recommended.

3.2 Important technical analysis patterns

Before exploring technical analysis (TA) in general, I just have a few brief remarks to make on the line styles used to portray data. More details can be found elsewhere, and in particular in the educational material of the company you use. I think the most informative lines are the "candlestick" types. If you like, this is a bit like a candle with the wick sticking out at each end. If the data are 5 min data for example, in each 5 minute period, the beginning and end data are indicated by the "solid" candle itself while the wick represents values attained during the 5 minute period for every data point. If the market has gone down during the period so far, the candle is one colour (usually red) while if it has gone up a different colour (e.g. green is used). With data coming in second by second, you can watch the solid region stretch and contract. You need to watch the markets to understand properly what is happening, but after a while you will see that understanding becomes second nature and you get an instant picture of how the market is moving. In the diagrams below, candlesticks are used but the "wicks" have been cut off to aid clarity.

Any financial market has certain common TA features which can be exploited in principle. These are of the form that if the chart pattern is a certain type, a particular change then takes place later. The chart patterns have special names associated with them, as follows. For a more detailed description, the reader is encouraged to explore resources available on the internet, for example, Investopedia have a concise guide together with good diagrams of chart patterns[7].

(i) Double top and bottom

Examples of a double top and a double bottom are shown in Figures 3.1 and 3.2. Essentially, in the case of a double top, the market has first peaked and then retreated. Later, prices increase again but do not exceed the previous value, and instead fall back. This is considered a bearish (i.e. prices are expected to decline) as the market has already psychologically set the upper limit for the price of the stock. In the case of a double bottom, the market has set some sort of minimum, which is a bullish sign (i.e. prices are expected to increase). Sometimes prices reverse again and you get a triple top or bottom. This is even more bearish or bullish respectively. For the price to be confirmed as a sell or buy, the price needs to move a distance beyond the confirmation point indicated in the diagram. However, in short time scale trading, a few hours or less, waiting for this confirmation may be too late. A common way of identifying these features is that they look like the letter W (double bottom) or its inversion (double top).

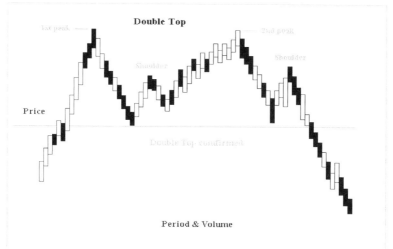

Figure 3.1. A double top in a stock price and its confirmation. Image by Altafqadar available from Wikipedia commons [8].

Figure 3.2. A double top in a stock price and its confirmation. Image by Altafqadar available from Wikipedia commons [8].

(ii) Head and shoulders

Figure 3.3. A head and shoulders formation in a stock price and its confirmation. Image by Altafqadar available from Wikipedia commons [9].

  Head and shoulders is not the shampoo but a chart formation, less easily identified than a double top or bottom. Figure 3.3 is the more conventional form with the head forming the main peak and two "shoulders" on either side. Figure 3.4 is an inverted head and shoulders formation. For the formation to be "confirmed" the price has to move beyond the "neckline". In this case, the formation is bearish while the inverted head and shoulders formation is bullish. Again, for the head and shoulders formation, after the main peak or trough, the argument is that the market psychology is half-hearted for subsequent peaks which is a bearish signal.

26

Investing by Spread Betting, by John Austin

Figure 3.4. A head and shoulders formation in a stock price and its confirmation. Image by Altafqadar available from Wikipedia commons [9].

Similar arguments apply to the inverted head and shoulders formation (Figure 3.4) which is a bullish signal.

(iii) Other patterns

Other useful chart patterns include *cup and handle, triangles, flags* and *pennants*. These are well described elsewhere, e.g. [7,10].

For a cup and handle formation, the chart pattern has a bowl-like shape leading to a peak. The price then retreats slightly before resuming its upward trend. This is a bullish signal. Often, instead of the pattern showing a price retreat, the price will pause before resuming its upward trend. The opposite pattern – an inverted cup and handle – is a bearish signal.

Triangles, flags and pennants are similar to each other. Often, after a period of rapid movement, the price variability will drop. This leads to an oscillation in price near the new price level.

After a period of time, the price might suddenly move one way or the other. A break-out above the general triangular shape is a bullish signal while a break-out below is a bearish sign.

(iv) Resistance and support levels

Useful TA indicators include *support* and *resistance* levels. As its name implies, the support level of the market represents the lower price limit. In a static market, if the price drops below support, then more buying is encouraged which keeps the price at the support level or above. Prices tend to go up near the support price. The opposite happens at the resistance level, where, in a static market, increases encourage more selling. For example for the head and shoulders formation, the support level is the neckline. Once a support line is breached, downwards, then the price tends to drop further and the old support level tends to become a new resistance level. The opposite is true when break out above the resistance level occurs. So, there is a tendency for resistance to become support and support to become resistance in bullish and bearish conditions respectively. You can get a good indication of the support and resistance levels of a given stock by simply looking at the past chart. Of course these are not always foolproof trading indications: sometimes a price will move slightly through a support level and then bounce back. The Bollinger bands and the Moving Average (see Chapter 3.3) give useful indicators of current resistance and support levels.

Best of luck with all that, as identifying the above chart patterns in real time is a lot more difficult than it looks!

3.3 Useful technical analysis tools

The charts tell you one thing, but it is essential to use other indicators before making a trade. Fortunately, spread betting companies offer a wide range of diagnostics to choose from, and you can overlay these on the stock price for live trading. Most traders have their pet diagnostics that they like to use, and IG for example give over 20 which can be presented on 15 timescales. It is easy to be overwhelmed, which is another reason why you may need several months' practice before establishing a trading strategy.

As a simple person, I like to keep things as simple as possible. I use the Bollinger bands, MACD and perhaps one or two more such as momentum or RSI. Typically, I use the 5 min data switching occasionally to 1 min in times of rapid change. I also look at the 1 day data to formulate a general strategy for a few days ahead. Examples of these charts for one trade that I had running on 29 July 2015 are given in the next few pages, but I will first describe the diagnostics themselves. Further details are available from the spread betting companies themselves.

(i) MACD

This is short for moving average convergence divergence. It was invented in the 1970s[11]. The idea is to have moving averages over different timescales and by comparing the values you can see at a glance whether the price is moving up or down. This is a useful way of smoothing out the noise in the stock price. The time scales usually chosen are 12, 26 and 9 periods of the base unit. Thus, if the chart is the 1 minute chart, the two main averages are over 12 and 26 min, while for the 1 day chart, the averages are over 12 and 26 days. The 12 period timescale gives a more immediate figure. If the market is increasing then that value will be higher than the 26 period figure.

The precise calculation is somewhat involved, so it is convenient that you don't have to do it yourself. The procedure starts with the 12 period average, which is not a simple arithmetic average but an exponential moving average (EMA). Rather than go into details here, the interested reader can obtain the mathematical details from [12]. A slower time scale average is taken from the 26 period EMA. In the charts themselves, the 26 period figure is subtracted from the 12 period figure and is typically shown in blue and marked as the MACD line. The third time scale used is typically 9 periods. The MACD itself is averaged using the EMA weighting factors over the 9 periods, and this gives the "signal line" often shown in red. Thus the signal line is the average of an average. In the absence of a trend, high recent values will start to decrease, and the blue and red lines will converge towards each other. This is a sell signal. In time the lines may cross over and go further apart so that the longer term value is higher than the short term value. Later, that will also turn around and the two lines will start to converge again. This time, though, with the blue line below the red line, this is a buying signal. Traditionally, a strict buy signal is not supposed to occur until the lines actually cross. This is often overcautious and will result in a significant reduction in profits. However, I know that I have a tendency to open trades a little early, so my little refinements should be treated with caution! Generally, the MACD like other diagnostics, are smoothed and can be expected to change gradually. This makes it easier to see when the various diagnostics have peaked or troughed which helps to make a trade at near enough the right time.

The presence of a trend complicates the situation. If the trend is up, over a multi-hour time scale, then the blue line may approach the red line from above, which might ordinarily be considered a sell, but the stock price often treads water at that stage or even rises slightly, depending on the strength of the trend. For convenience, the difference between the red and blue lines is indicated by a set of histograms: expanding histograms above the zero line implies a buy, expanding histograms below the zero line suggests a sell. In the full charts, the histograms themselves are colour coded so that the picture can be seen instantly. The diagrams I show in the print version of this book are grey scale figures, but the original colour diagrams can be seen on my website[13] or in the electronic version.

The time scale is very relevant, as different time scales will give a different picture. I generally find that the 5 min. charts are most useful, except possibly in rapid trading at the market opening. For much of the time, use of the MACD diagnostic can give one picture but then turn around very quickly. So use of the 5 minute diagnostics generally allows some sort of confirmed signal to be established. In principle, the timescales of 12, 26 and 9 periods can be adjusted, but this could be quite confusing. The time scales were originally chosen before instant data were available and were based on daily data. In this case, the timescales refer to two weeks, one month and one and a half weeks once allowance is made for the weekend trading lull. In principle, other time scales might therefore be more appropriate, particularly for day trading, but the 12, 26, 9 periods have become so established that the diagnostics computed with them have probably become a self-fulfilling prophecy.

(ii) Bollinger bands and the moving average

This is a fancy name for the typical range of the stock market price[14] and involve two parameters N and K. The moving average is a simple moving average of the price which would be constant in the absence of any trend. The averaging period is the first of the two parameters (*N*, typically 20). The Bollinger bands are a set number of standard deviation departures from the moving average. The number of standard deviations is given by the second parameter. When the parameter *K* is 2, if prices are normally distributed, then 95% of the time the price will remain Between the Bollinger bands. They provide useful levels of support and resistance, as noted in Chapter 3.2. When the market is not trending, the upper Bollinger band provides resistance and the lower Bollinger band provides support. If the price is trending upwards, the moving average tends to provide support, while if the price is trending downwards, the moving average tends to provide resistance. During quiet times, the price will appear to converge towards the moving average (of course it's really the other way around).

This Bollinger bands are not particularly reliable as support and resistance level indicators during relatively quiet market conditions, because the standard deviation of the price can change suddenly. One way of avoiding getting confused by false signals is to look at the charts for different time periods.

(iii) Momentum

Although I do plot it, I do not always find it useful. The momentum indicator indicates the "speed of movement" of the price. It is the average difference between closing and opening prices for the last few periods. The number of periods chosen can be changed, but is typically 12. When the price has been generally increasing during the periods, the momentum is positive and is negative when the price has been decreasing. One of the ideas in using it, is to relate to the physical principle of "conservation of momentum", with the idea that once a stock is moving in a particular direction, it will keep doing so, at least for a while. However, to my mind this doesn't work at all like the rigorous physics principle so it is a matter of *caveat emptor*.

(iv) Relative Strength Index

The RSI measures whether stocks are generally increasing or decreasing based on opening and closing prices for each period[15]. Typically, a 14 period time scale is applied and the index is a measure of the number of rises during the period to the number of falls. The ratio is expressed as a percentage. High and low values are 70 and 30 respectively. When the value is high, the price can be monitored for signs of a decrease in the ratio and of an equivalent reversal in the recent rises. When the RSI is low, a price increase may be implicated. While interesting to look at from time to time, I find this diagnostic generally to be less revealing than others such as the MACD: by the time that the RSI has retreated, for example, the price has already typically dropped significantly.

There are some rather banal practicalities in drawing the charts. In principle it is easy to have a large number of technical analysis tools written on the chart. Mostly, though, these take space away from the main stock price. So, as you increase the number of diagnostics, the main chart steadily shrinks in height and making out the movements becomes increasingly challenging. Of course having the extra diagnostics available means that you tend to spend time looking at them and this can slow down your reaction to market changes. I think Bollinger bands are essential, plus just one or two other diagnostics for highest efficiency. Of those MACD provides the most information, in my humble view. You might also like to include momentum or RSI. The former is convenient because it is close to MACD in the alphabetic list of TA tools!

3.4 Example of a Trade in Progress

The example below shows a trade that I had just opened about half an hour before I printed the chart. Figure 3.5 shows the 5 minute data while Figures 3.6 and 3.7 show the daily and 1 minute data respectively. Each chart provides a different perspective. Note first of all, the considerable detail in the chart illustrating how a full size computer screen is especially useful to see the details, which unfortunately, will be difficult to make out in the print version of this book (but is clear in the e-book version). For the full size image and full colour display, the reader is invited to download the free diagrams from my website[13].

When the trade was opened, I used the 5 min chart (Figure 3.5). This shows that after an upward movement. The FTSE 100 dipped slightly just before 8 am and this was reflected in the reduction of the MACD histograms at the bottom of the chart. The histograms then started to increase again and so I went long at 6594. There was a lot of noise soon afterward, characteristic of official market opening, and the price continued its upward trend with the MACD histograms following in step. By about 8.30 am my profit was around £20, but prices were still volatile. In this chart, the opening trade is indicated by the thick line across the chart,

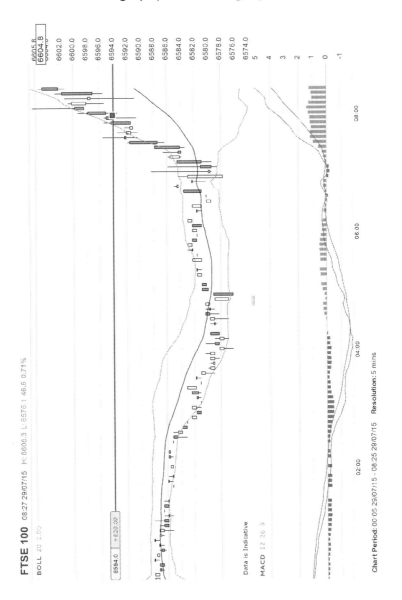

Figure 3.5 Trade in progress (FTSE100 long at 6594). Five minute data through IG markets.

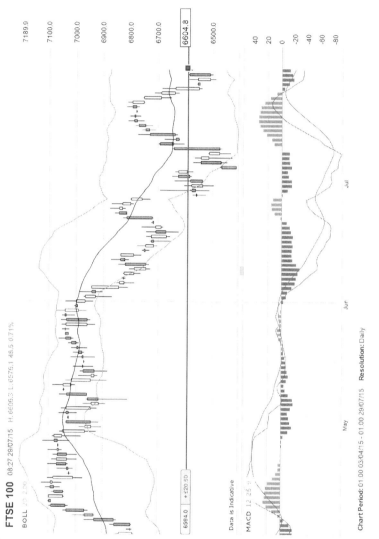

Figure 3.6 Trade in progress (FTSE100 long at 6594). Daily data through IG markets.

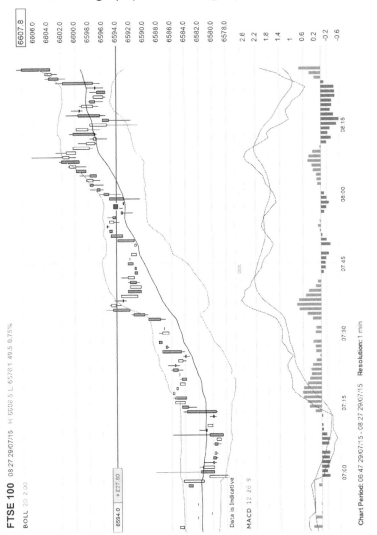

Figure 3.7 Trade in progress (FTSE100 long at 6594). One minute data through IG markets.

and the running profit is shown within a small box on the left. Hovering the mouse over that box brings up another box allowing

36

the position to be closed immediately. This is very useful for rapid trades. In the time that it took me to print the charts, the profit went from £20 to £27!

On the daily charts, Figure 3.5, the MACD histograms are negative and decreasing in size suggesting overall a future increase in the share price. Several days later, the FTSE100 was near 6700, and close to the multi-day moving average line. The one minute data apparently indicates less randomness. After the market peak at 8.08 am. The price dropped to the 6596 level before surging to over 6607. These moves are reflected in the MACD histograms, which turn from negative to positive at 8.01 am and then again at 8.24 am.

Unfortunately, I didn't close my position there, but I let it run further. The market actually then retreated and I closed my position with a £10 loss! I had become somewhat mesmerised by the price movements and failed to engage my brain, a not unusual situation. It shows the need for vigilance. Also, virtually every trade is sub-optimal and there is nearly always another 5-10 points on the table. However, providing significant profits are obtained, there is no point in becoming over concerned about missed opportunities.

3.5 Automatic trading systems

You could instead wash your hands of all this TA confusion and subscribe to automatic trading alerts[6], as noted in the Introduction of this Chapter. Unfortunately, there are many financial people whose main task is to part you from your hard-earned as quickly as possible. You have to remember, though, that past systems are tuned to previous data, and in producing a given share index model, there will be many adjustable parameters. The code writers will then have gone through these parameters adjusting their values until they get the best reproduction of the market. For example, the writers might obtain 10 years of stock market data and use the first 5 years to determine the best fit of the parameters. They then might apply the same parameters for the next 5 years and choose the model which gives the best results. There is no guarantee of course that the same model will work in the future. In presenting the "performance" of a particular system, you will only see the best result, not the myriad of other models that don't work well. Nonetheless, the computer will come up with a better prediction than your or I can possibly get just from looking at the chart and technical analysis.

In view of their potentially superior performance, you might want to use them instead, so here are some of the problems. Of course in calculating your profits you need to price in the cost of the subscription service and here are some less quantifiable issues.

(i) Is the information timely?

Depending on the communication methods, you might find out the recommendation 5 minutes after the signal has been highlighted. This is perhaps less of a problem now than it was, as most people seem to be connected by the hip to their mobile phones. Nonetheless, any delay can result in loss of performance in a fast moving market such as the Dow.

(ii) Have you traded according to the instructions?

This seems easy. How difficult can it be to do what you're told? Actually it's very difficult. When the market is tanking, are you able to go long? If the market seems close to its peak can you still buy? If you have a reasonable profit already, can you resist closing your position to realise your gain? If you have a large paper loss that looks to be increasing, are you able to hold on for dear life?

(iii) Is the system you're subscribing to really any good?

The trouble is that you never really know what you're getting. All systems have been trained against past data, so success in the future may be less assured. Some trades you make will go to a loss. If you buy into a system which starts to win from the beginning, then that is half the battle towards accepting an automated system. But if your system loses from the beginning, what do you do next?

Very often, instructions come without explanation and so you are left in the dark, or alternately, the reasons for a trade are so shrouded in stock market jargon that they seem unintelligible. By all means give it a go, but personally I prefer to be in "control", even if I make a mess of it from time to time. I have the delusion (if that's what it is) that I will get better!

4. What and When to Trade

4.1 Introduction

What and when to trade are personal choices that boil down to what you find most comfortable. You can of course trade individual stocks, but these have a large spread and making money on these can entail a lot of knowledge or perhaps some insider information. Using insider information is of course illegal, but few prosecutions ever seem to occur, and according to one ex-banker, some obnoxious professionals consider insider dealing to be no worse than "pissing in a swimming pool"[16]. For you and I it may take individual stocks over a day to move the distance of the spread. The time scale over which you can trade then rather depends on the variance in the share price compared with the spread. Variance is a statistical measure of the variability of the stock. You can get hold of this information by plotting the "Bollinger bands" on the chart for the stock, as noted in the previous Chapter. Individual FTSE100 stocks generally have smaller spreads than medium or small cap shares, but they can also be less variable. The time of day to trade depends on your personal preference, but there is often most activity as the market opens and as the market closes, but the down side of this is that it can all be a bit chaotic, particularly in the morning, so you may be caught out by a spike in the share price. One reason that you are never going to make a fortune share trading or spread betting is that you are too nice a person to do insider trading, but there is probably no reason that you can't make a reasonable living if that's what you want. In practice, the time to trade depends on the market chosen.

4.2 Indices

Rather than trading commodities or individual stocks which might have a spread of more than 2%, for day trading you need to seek out those markets which have a very small spread, which includes indices such as the FTSE100, Dow, Dax etc. The spread on the FTSE100 from IG markets is 1 pt during market hours (0.014%) while the Dow is even smaller (1.8 pts in 18,000, or 0.01%). The Bollinger bands are typically ± 2 standard deviations from the mean, and generally, with no overall trend, you can expect a movement, say from the lower to the upper Bollinger band. This means that this distance, indicated on the charts, will need to be at least 10 times the spread to obtain a decent profit. Of course during trends, the trend rate may be more important than the Bollinger bands. Personally, I find that the Dow moves too quickly for my taste. Although it is often possible for me to see potential profits, by the time I think of making a move, the market has already moved and I become paralysed by indecisiveness. The S&P 500, which is a more broadly-based index is my preference when I want a position on the US market.

There are several times per day when there is likely to be market variability. Two particular times are as the market opens in the morning (and there are sometimes two opportunities) given by the European market at 7 am and the UK market at 8 am. There is an initial froth on the market, during the first 5 minutes of trading in particular when changes are very rapid. There are opportunities to trade the FTSE100 here often as much as 10 or 15 points even in a flat market. You have to be prepared to get in and out very quickly, though, within 5 or 10 minutes, as the prices can swing violently. Once the general trend, if any, has been established, there may be good opportunities to trade for an hour or two. On many days, the market then settles down and the Bollinger bands may become too close together to trade intelligently. A second important time to consider is about 2.30 pm UK time, when the US market opens and can trigger sympathetic movements in the FTSE. Another major trading opportunity often exists in late afternoon as final prices for the day are being set. Other opportunities occur at different times, which are somewhat random and are worth watching for. However, I often find myself missing these chances because I have become bored watching the market and I've gone off for lunch or something!

One particular index that should not be dismissed is the China 300 index, or to give it its full name, the Shanghai Shenzhen 300 stock index futures, the index of the leading 300 Chinese shares. During market hours, the IG spread is 3 points in about 4000, or 0.075%, much larger than the FTSE or Dow. However, it is not unusual for the market to move 50 or 60 points in a relatively short time. At the IG minimum volume of £5/pt you could end up gaining (or losing) several hundred pounds in less than an hour. It can be a bit of a knuckle duster ride, but if you're prepared to take the risk, the reward is potentially there. Of course the market opens at night, at about 2 am and closes soon after 8 am. Outside these hours the market spread goes from 3 to 12 points. So, if you make a trade with the minimum volume in the off-market, your position goes £60 down the tubes before you even start. This would need to be a long term trade to be worthwhile. Nonetheless, I have successfully traded before 7 am when the market spread is tolerable. You can even consider working nights and trade the Chinese market between 2 and 8 am, if you become really serious about your trading. The China 300 often goes through large movements of 10 or 20 points at various times, usually some time after the market opens, occasionally at other times, as well as 6 am to 8 am.

4.3 Forex

Foreign exchange (Forex) of the major currencies is also worth considering. For example. The £/$ exchange rate spread is 2 points in 15000, but although the spread is similar to the FTSE, the latter has more variability and has the potential for higher profits. When I started trading, though, I tried the exchange rate because it was less risky, and it provides a useful platform for testing trading ideas. Generally, I found this to be successful and then later I moved on to the FTSE100 primarily.

Unlike the major stock indices for which the "blind faith" strategy (buy and hold) can work effectively, this won't generally work for forex, which is both strongly influenced by politics, and in general you cannot expect a long term trend. For this reason, forex is probably best reserved for day trading. One of the possible advantages of switching to forex in the summer is that the indices have a tendency to become less predictable. One argument is that exchange rates are determined by the large international movements of capital, which continue during the summer regardless. Consequently, speculative investors are less able to shift the exchange rates in their favour.

4.4 Practical Trading

I have found that the same technical analysis tools are generally effective in all the markets I've tried. Hence, if you become comfortable with, say the FTSE100, transferring your understanding to another market should be straightforwards. The main differences are the timings of major moves and the potential gain compared with the size of the spread. Some markets are even well-correlated, such as the FTSE100 and the Dow. During the off-market, this can be quite uncanny with the FTSE100 moving with the Dow while the US market is still open. For this reason you might even consider trading the FTSE up until the US market closes. Although FTSE market spread is higher, its reduced noise

44

compared with the Dow may be sufficient compensation. A plausible strategy is to trade uncorrelated markets at different times. I have done that with the China 300 before 7 am and the FTSE afterwards. Sometimes, China stocks induce variability in the FTSE, but more typically, the Shanghai market provides significant trading opportunities while the London market is awaiting its official opening.

One word of caution: whenever a market moves in one direction or another, due for example to political news, a step function might then occur in the price. The technical analysis may not be very reliable under these conditions because their interpretation usually assumes a steadily varying price. For example, there could be a downward movement following a political announcement. The market might then move 1 or 2% down in 15 minutes. The MACD analysis might imply that the market is pointing downwards, whereas in reality it may now be constant relative to the new (lower) price. For the diagnostics to be reliable, you might need to wait an hour, but by then trading opportunities might be lost. Technical analysis is a guide, not a rigorous science!

Investing by Spread Betting, by John Austin

5. Some Clichés and a Mantra

5.1 Introduction

The stock market abounds with sayings of various kinds, which in practice are bordering on the meaningless, as we shall see. Typically these are the style of yin and yang, take profits but leave some for the next person; etc. etc. These ideas can be ensconced in a mantra that you can work with, but of course you will need some practice putting the ideas into practice, or indeed seeing the circumstances in which you can profitably break your own rules, which might be useful from time to time.

Also, I expect you have read stock market reports which "explain" why the market has gone up or down. Again, this is quite meaningless at times, but with a mantra you can give yourself the satisfaction of a reason for success or failure. It reminds me a bit like my old school teacher who, talking of (A-level) organic chemistry said that: you can explain everything but predict nothing! Your goal is to use everything at your disposal, even tacky sayings to predict the future behaviour of *something*, anything will do!

Here is a set of sayings, and what, they might mean. You can compose a mantra based on those that you find most useful. It helps to remind yourself of your mantra from time to time, as it is easy to be caught up in the moment!

5.2 Some stock market clichés

1. TRADE WITH THE BRAIN NOT THE HEART[17]

You can examine the situation as much as you like, but unless you make the trade it's all academic. Unfortunately, the act of trading creates an emotional attachment to your money and by inference the position you have set up! The purpose of the technical analysis and all other prior price analyses is to try to get an objective idea of likely future market moves, which helps to reduce the emotional element. So, once you have done the analysis, make the trade! Often while the trade is running, the circumstances change. Once you are certain that the latest TA goes against your trade, then the logical thing to do is to seek an exit at the earliest opportunity. Doing this of course is easier said than done and is arguably one of the faults I have in trading. It is coupled to the idea of cutting your losses early (point 4: Cut your losses quickly). Often when I open a trade I get an immediate emotional response. If the market has already eliminated the spread, then I feel confident, if the price has moved slightly against me, my reaction is to think I have made a mistake! However, this is short term froth and I know I need to relax.

Another aspect of the emotional attachment is that there is always a temptation to respond near instantly to market moves. See also points 2 (Wait for a signal confirmation before trading) and 3 (Before trading, check all the relevant TA signals). With our computers we can easily do that. There are some circumstances when this might be appropriate such as a rapidly moving early market. It takes experience to work out when a rapid response is potentially profitable. This requires some thought, i.e. using the brain, not the emotions. There is also a corresponding situation in closing a trade. Often the market spikes and this can increase profits or suddenly increase the losses. Depending on our decision in opening the trade, it might be that our limit or mental stop loss might be triggered. There is probably no harm in responding if there has been a surge in profit, as you may well get the chance to reopen the trade at a better price. These situations can occur more often in the off-market when volume is necessarily lower. The best strategy would be on the lookout for spikes and take advantage accordingly. Often, once the price has spiked up, say, in a few seconds, it will spike back down again on the same time scale. Just bear this in mind and take care! Or, as Corporal Jones in Dad's Army used to say, while appearing to be panicking, "Don't Panic, don't panic....". Another set of circumstances in which emotions run high is when you have just closed a trade for other reasons, not just a spike.

If you have made a loss, on the position, there is tremendous motivation to make up for it by reversing your previous position or reopening it. Reopening it may actually be sensible as long as it is on the basis of the evidence in front of you, which can only be the technical analysis. For example, suppose you have opened a short and the market has surged up, so you have quickly closed your short and gone long instead. Now the market reverses! So, you have lost money on the way up, and lost money on the way down! Unfortunately, if you let your emotions get the better of you, this can easily occur. Sometimes the best strategy when you have made any trade, winning or losing, is to walk away and come back in 15 minutes. There will then be new information for you to digest and you can approach the next trade (if any) with a fresh perspective. Note the use in the last sentence of the qualifier "if any". By all means as a mental exercise make predictions as to how the market is about to move. But you don't *have to trade*: you *can* sit on the sidelines and wait (see point 10: Trade only when there is a strong chance of a profit).

2. WAIT FOR A SIGNAL CONFIRMATION BEFORE TRADING[18]

Having decided what signal to use to make a trade, you need to "confirm" that the signal is working. In other words you need to see the price going down to "confirm" a sell signal, but this is a basic requirement as the price could increase again very quickly. For example, you might use a decreasing MACD histogram as the trading signal to sell. If you use a 1 minute signal you might get one result, but the 1 min signal can change very quickly. Don't forget: the TA is a result of the trades, not the other way around! If you use the 5 min signal, then the MACD data will become available at a given time. You may still need to allow several minutes to ensure that the direction of the MACD does not change again. One way that you can do this in principle is to use the 5 min signal make up your mind that "yes, I'm going to buy/sell in the next few minutes" then switch to the 1 min data to optimise the timing. What can often happen is that if the time is right, the spread will be eliminated within a few seconds of the position being opened, at least for a small spread quantity like the FTSE100. It will take a little bit of experience before you can comfortably make these decisions, and even then, there is still some doubt, as every trade has an uncertain outcome to a degree.

3. BEFORE TRADING CHECK ALL THE RELEVANT TA SIGNALS

Hopefully you will have already have been monitoring your favourite technical analysis tools simultaneously such as the Bollinger bands and the MACD histograms over different time scales. Whether the stock is about to set new values for the day or whether there are other "resistance points" should be considered. For example, the price often stalls near the moving average. You might in principle take this opportunity to bail out (lower risk strategy). Likewise, a lower risk strategy is to bail out of a buy near the top of the positive Bollinger band, or bail out of a sale at the negative Bollinger band. If you are feeling adventurous, you might hold for a little longer. If the price is about to make a significant move, it may go beyond either of the Bollinger bands. In principle, you can consider buying above the positive Bollinger band (or selling below the negative Bollinger band) but before you do that you need some sort of evidence that the price is likely to move. For example, a "significant" movement away from the previous price range.

4. CUT YOUR LOSSES QUICKLY[19]

This is one of the most difficult and frustrating ideas to implement and is coupled with the general idea of exactly when do you throw in the towel in a losing trade? The trade will presumably have been opened on the basis of TA signals of some kind, so the first thing to do is to check that those signals are still doing what you expect. The obvious solution is to close the position if things have changed, but this is too simplistic. For example, you might lose £20 in the first 5 minutes if things have gone badly, but thereafter the position could stabilise before reversing. If you were to look at the position before the price starts reversing again, you might not think of trading at all. In other words for example, the psychological influence of a price surge within the last 5 minutes would tend to discourage a sell (see point 8). That has happened to me: I've gone short, the position moves against me and I've closed only to see the position turn around. I'm then paralysed and unable to reopen my short. If I had stayed in the market I would have achieved a profit instead of a loss. Once recording a loss, one is often reluctant to get back into the market again. In particular one of the things I've noticed is for the tendency of the market to become very volatile prior to a major move. For example you might be short, the market surges upwards you then panic and close, and the market oscillates wildly before tanking. This brings us back to point 1 (Trade with the brain not the heart). Well, when do you know when to cut your losses early as suggested? You don't, you only know it in hindsight! It just helps to know how your chosen market behaves, and that may take several months of intensive trading. I would say that this is one of my major trading faults, and I need to keep reminding myself of it, which is why it is listed in my mantra.

5. LET YOUR PROFITS RUN[20]

Don't be too quick to close a position that is in profit. A share that is expensive can get more expensive; one that is cheap can get cheaper. There is another stock market aphorism (the other side of the yin and yang if you like) as equally meaningless as this one: leave something for the next man. In other words, leave some profit on the table for the next person. But why should you? If the market has gone up a long way and somebody is daft enough to be buying still, let them! Often, though, you might be panicked into closing your position early. For example, the market has a tendency to stall and perhaps even go into reverse as the price reaches the moving average. [This moving average varies with the chart time scale, so if you're using the 5 min candlesticks, then the moving average will be an average over typically 20 periods, or 100 minutes.] Under these conditions, you could find your profit evaporating rapidly and there is some risk that it will disappear entirely as the market goes into a real reverse. More often though, the volatility will settle and the prior direction will resume. I don't personally like this situation. I find it too stressful if I am watching carefully, so I tend to close once the price reaches the moving average. I then sit on the sidelines and curse my bad decision! So, I'm not really running with my profits. However, I am to a degree. I used to be much worse, closing before the end of the 5 min period. Now I usually wait until the end of the period before seeing how things are going. That is still too early, though, and it's a bad combination not to run with my wins and not to close my losses early. Sometimes I get it right, and the sometimes is enough to ensure a profit, at least to date!

6. DO NOT TRADE IN THE "off-market"

The FTSE market closes at 4.30 pm, after which the spread increases from 1 to 2 points. At 9pm the spread in the unofficial market goes to 5 pts and remains there until 7 am the following morning. Trading between 4.30 pm and 9 pm can be profitable, as the US market is open, and there is still some price variability to exceed the spread. Except in unusual circumstances you cannot necessarily expect the market to move enough to justify the 5 pt spread. In addition, as the market volume is much lower, market movements are somewhat unpredictable. However, if you have good reason to trade, for example, there is major political news, by all means go ahead. For example, I have traded the Sunday FTSE offered by IG and made a £60 profit even though the spread was 10 pts. I did this during July 2015 while the situation in Greece was uncertain. I also traded immediately after the results from exit poles were announced following the 2015 UK election. Generally, though, I try to trade the FTSE only between 7 am and 5 pm, Monday to Friday, but boring old fart like I am, I often watch the market at other times. Obviously there are exceptions to the general rule. Sometimes the market will trend over quite a range early in the morning and it may be worth taking the risk even with a 5 pt spread. Usually, these trends are rapid but short-lived, so you can pick up 15 pts in 15 minutes. It is always worth watching the market at 7 am. Often, the market will surge up at 7 am only to reverse entirely 5 minutes later (or the other way around). If you have a strong enough constitution there is money to be had there, and with the spread dropping to 2 pts there is a lower cost and an increased chance of making some profit.

Similar principles apply to other markets, and you need to get the experience in your chosen market to make the correct judgement. If you want to reduce the problem of off-market trading then you can in principle, trade around the world, starting with the Shanghai or Tokyo market in the early hours of the morning, shifting to the European market and then to the US markets. You can then get 4 hours' sleep per night and catch up at the weekend! This is a bit obsessional! Are you a professional, or something?

7. DO NOT TRADE THE FTSE100 DURING THE MIDDLE OF THE DAY

The problem during the middle of the day is that the share price variance drops. This means that when you open a position there can be a long time before the price moves significantly (one way or the other). It can be a good time to open a position if you are trading for the multi-day timescale and you can then be sure that the froth of the early morning market has dissipated. However, even trading for the multi-day timescale you might try to time the opening of your positions. The way to obtain the market variance at a glance is to look at the Bollinger bands at the current time for the short timescales, say one minute. The difference between the upper and lower bands might be less than 10 points, so you know that even with good timing you're unlikely to pick up much more than 5 points, compared with the spread of 1. This may be enough of course, but the variations are a bit random, and you might suddenly find yourself on the wrong side of a trade. While the reduction in market variance often occurs between about 10 am and 3 pm, it can occur at any time. Even between those hours there could be an overall trend in the FTSE which you might be able to take advantage of.

8. DON'T CHASE THE MARKET[21]

This is a very important principle. The reasons why you should not in general chase the market is that it lowers your potential gains while increasing the potential risk should the market price reverse. For example, if you see the market surging very rapidly, the chances are that this could be a spike and the price will drop down again shortly. If you've bought on the spike, then the subsequent drop will leave your position significantly underwater and you may be lucky to get out with a profit. It is not always easy to recognise these features, but if you are watching the market, you will get an idea of the natural time scale over which variations are occurring at the time you're watching. If there is a sudden change in time scale, then you have to be suspicious. Also, the market nearly always overdoes it: both upward and downward movements are too large. So, after a rapid, sustained loss, you can expect the market to turn around and retrace its steps, at least a little. These little steps may be enough to pick up some money against the general market trend. However, during days with sustained trends, it is often difficult knowing when to enter the market. It is a bit like jumping aboard a moving train! At times the market will pause and in principle this could be an opportunity to get in. There is a danger, though, that the market has reached its maximum or minimum and is heading in reverse. So, if the market has been dropping, then opening a short during one period when the market seems to pause, is potentially hazardous.

9. TRADE WITH THE MARKET NOT AGAINST[22]

If the market is decreasing, then opening a long can generally be expected to separate you from your cash very quickly. This goes against the idea of the price of other objects: if they are cheap, then they're a bargain. The stock market, though works differently. Market prices are largely arbitrary: a stock price is just the price at which the buyers and sellers are balanced, it implies nothing about the fundamental value of a stock. There are certain constraints of course in that if the p/e of a stock is 20, it implies a 5% per annum earnings, which is currently much larger than fixed investment returns, such as cash on deposit. So owning the stock gives a better rate of return than safer investments which are not as risky and the higher return compensates for the higher risk. Apart from that, share prices could change by 10% or more without affecting the basic arguments. The release of news tends to trigger changes in share prices which in turn affect the share indices. Once prices start dropping the psychology of the market tends to trigger more sales.

It follows that in the short term, trading the opposite way to the market leads to rapid losses. Unfortunately, it is not always easy to see what the direction of the market is, whatever the time scale of the trade. Perhaps one of the main reasons that I lost money in the past is my disregard for this rule, or perhaps thinking that although the market is down, it will soon reverse. Often, prices will change very quickly, and then you need an exit strategy: when do you close the position? This is one of the most difficult decision to make and relates to point 4 (Cut your losses quickly) of when to close a losing position.

10. TRADE ONLY WHEN THERE IS A STRONG CHANCE OF A PROFIT

There is no harm of course in having an opinion at any time regarding the way the market will move in the next half hour or so, even if this is just a mental exercise. Sooner or later, though, you have to commit funds and it makes sense to do this when you have most chance of making a profit. While it is always difficult to know whether a particular trade will result in a profit, you can maximise your chances with the application of TA principles. Obviously, this doesn't guarantee a success. With practice, probably three quarters or more of your trades can be profitable. The numbers of wins to losses doesn't so much matter as the gain or loss each time. The temptation is to close the wins early, to guarantee a profit, but to hang on for dear life when the trade is going downhill. So, if you're not careful the amount lost in the losing trades may be larger than the amount won per trade in the profitable ones. Practice with real and imagined trades will help in the long term, and that is presumably why the first three months of my trading resulted in only break-even. The "imaginary" trades you should treat with proper rigour. Using a demo account would help here, but once you are up and running going back to a demo account is a strange thing to do. So, in the imaginary trades you should "open" the position at a particular time and then be sure not to back track if your hypothetical trade is sliding. It's still not money of course and it is not always easy to transfer the dispassionate approach of a demo account or an imaginary trade without a lot of personal discipline. I still tend to close my positions too early, which does reduce the profit significantly. Nonetheless, you cannot expect to get more than a small amount, say one half of the available profit. It is important to do a postmortem for every trade, and companies like IG recommend that you keep a trading diary for this purpose. Hindsight, though, is a perfect science and there is no point in beating yourself up over missed opportunities or botched trades. Just try to learn for the future!

11. DON'T TRADE TOO OFTEN[23]

How long is a piece of string? Frequent trading with regular stocks can be expensive due to the cost of stamp duty as well as the market spread. With spread betting, there is no stamp duty to pay and the market spread is somewhat smaller, particularly for indices. This means that in practice, you can trade as frequently as you like. In my first three months of intensive trading, I was trading about 10 times per day (10 openings and closures). That was certainly too many times for me because my success rate was relatively low at 50%. At times I was getting caught up in the action instead of sitting back and seeing how best to profit from a particular situation. In my "training" period, I have learnt the best times to trade and what works best for me, subject to my personal weaknesses, primarily a tendency to open early and close too early. All you need is two good trades per day picking up 10 points each time. At the minimum of £2 per point you can make £40 per day trading primarily in the morning and evening rush hour! If three quarters of the trades are successful then you will pick up a net £20 per day. This is not a huge amount, but it scales up with the risk that you are prepared to take. At £5 per point, the profit becomes £50 per day while risking about £50 per day on average. Of course these are very crude averages, depending on market conditions. Some days, you may only be able to break even other days you might gain 100 points. For the large profits, though, you need to let your profits run (point 5), but I'm not very good at that!

12. TIMING NOT TIME

This actually turns around the usual stock market saying[24]. If you trade for the long term then your spread betting account might as well be a standard share account but with the facility to go short and extra gearing. Suppose, though, that you don't care about small fluctuations but you have just decided to trade and hold, for example by buying an index or a FTSE share in your spread betting account. Then it won't matter when you buy, just hold your position for a few years and reap the rewards. That's if you can resist the temptation to cash in if your account goes well in the black! You'll need the patience of a saint for this strategy as well as a lot of equity in your account if the index does go belly up. It is also an unbelievably dull strategy and is presumably not why you have a spread betting account.

If instead your thinking is, like mine, to build up capital over the long term by regular trading over the short term (" a long journey begins with the first step") then timing is the key. Obviously if you open a sell position and the index surges up then you're in trouble and you need an exit strategy. Usually, though, market movements take place on different time scales. It has often been jokingly said that a long term trade is a short term trade gone wrong! So, sometimes it may be best just to grin and bear it. You may be £100 down the tubes, but it's another day tomorrow! I have often closed large losing positions only to regret it a few hours later. There are no simple answers: it helps to be vigilant but the market can often move very quickly. A losing position is also a bit like the apocryphal experiment (at least I hope nobody does it anymore). You place a frog in a pan of cold water and slowly heat it: the frog boils to death instead of jumping to safety. Your position is the frog, slowly getting worse. Do you jump now (and risk not picking up money if the market turns), or do you hang on for dear life and hope things eventually improve? I must confess that I tend to do the latter, even though it is contrary to the recommended way (see point 4: Cut your losses quickly). The statistics I have done on my own trades indicate that I am nearly always right, after a fashion! The trouble is that I often close positions at a loss when a little more suffering would pay dividends.

It troubles me to some degree that my positions nearly always show some profit at some time, yet I don't always take the best advantage. In practice I don't realise that profit because I have closed at the wrong time. I don't claim to be particularly clever in being able to trade at a profit most of the time, if only in principle. Think of the thought experiment: choose a random time. Then go long or short on the FTSE, determined by a coin toss. What is the likelihood of making a profit? You might think of it as quite low. In reality, there is probably enough volatility that a random trade could show a profit. Questions to be asked are how long do you need to wait before the position is profitable, and can you stomach the bumpy ride along the way? Turning this idea to your advantage, then, perhaps if your position tanks then leaving it alone and walking away may well be the best strategy. I refer here of course to major indices (the Dow, FTSE etc.) and major foreign exchange rates for which the spreads are low and market movements are relatively sedate, except for the odd Black Monday[25]. Traders in individual stocks may be less fortunate!

There is another aspect of the "timing versus time" debate. The reason why in stock market investments one is generally advised to trade for the longer term and ignore short term volatility, is of course that timing is extremely difficult. However, the main reason for spread betting, at least as I see it, is to optimise timing to be able to trade for example in a flat but volatile market. You buy and close on the way up and short sell on the way down. The question of time scales, though is essentially the same conundrum. In regular share markets, the time scale is long (normally months or years) but in spread betting you have a range of time scales at your disposal, which for practical purposes range from minutes and above. So what time scale do you choose and how do you maximise profits? One would have thought that if you take care of the short time scale (sub one hour) then over several months your account will take care of itself. The problem is that as in trading in real shares, it is easy to be out of the market, or trading in the wrong direction when major moves occur. Also, as market moves occur, you might think that, if you are paying attention, then you will be able to scramble aboard. This never seems quite to work, at least in my case. Often nothing happens for hours, and then I am distracted or otherwise engaged when the market moves. It is then often difficult to find a point actually to return to the market (see point 15: The party may last longer than you expect). If you find you can easily climb aboard, the chances are that the party has ended and the market may be about to turn. It is here that we need reminding that technical analysis has only told you what has occurred. While an inference for the future is possible, this is not as accurate as a weather forecast! So although short term trading can work in principle, there is increased risk due to the noise in the data and you may not be in the market when positive changes occur. On the plus side, with short term trading you hopefully miss the times when the market would otherwise have moved against you. Whether one particular time scale is superior to another depends on the market itself, your own skills, your appetite for risk, the time of year and how much time you sit at your computer desk. This is probably going to take months for you to find out. You may never have definitive answers!

13. GO TO CASH AT THE END OF THE DAY

This is an idea for consideration rather than necessarily any positive recommendation. It is something I generally like to do as I like a (supposedly) lower risk strategy and I sleep better that way! On days that my trades have been swinging from positive to negative territory and back again it is a great relief to be unaffected by off-market movements. I can come fresh to my computer the following morning and make a trade without any baggage from the previous day. Often, though, a situation will present itself during off-market hours and I feel quite confident of the trade outcome. Under these circumstances, I might open a trade. Less successfully, I have been on the wrong side of a position and rather than close at a loss, I have sometimes run on overnight or even over the weekend in the hope that my position might improve.

Overnight you have to pay long or short interest, but this is quite small and amounts to £0.55 and £0.37 per point (with IG) respectively. If you think about it the former corresponds to an annual amount of £201 per point for the FTSE at 6700, or 3% per annum. Short interest is about 2% per annum, and both are not unreasonable. Of course if you are long of any stock you will be paid dividends at the appropriate date, while if you are short, then you will have to pay them. For the FTSE, this usually works out at about £4 per week although it is very variable and is not paid every week. If you trade on short time scales as I often do, you might need to take account of the dividends. For the FTSE these are paid or payable on Wednesdays immediately after the official market closes. Once the dividend is paid, the FTSE drops an equivalent number of points, perhaps as much as 5 points. In principle, whether the dividend is paid or not should not make any difference. However, it must have a psychological element. In other words, a sudden drop in the FTSE price could encourage more sales which might take a little time to catch up. Also, I don't know if investors buy specifically for the dividend. So in principle, the price of the FTSE could go up shortly before the close of play. These issues have concerned me from time to time, and for small trades where you are looking for 5-10 points or so, it may be better to avoid trading late in the afternoon session on Wednesdays. If you close your position 1 second before the 4.30 pm deadline, then you don't get the dividend (long position) nor do you pay it (short position).

14. YOU'RE ONLY ONE TRADE AWAY FROM DISASTER[26]

In principle, you are indeed only one trade away from making a big loss. However, my experience is rather that things go well for a while and there is a period of regress or treading water. With any luck you make more money during the good times to pay for the bad times! This happens with regular share trading as well of course, but with spread betting I always feel as if I am on the edge of my seat and losses will systematically add up. This has a tendency to affect confidence and encourages bad investment decisions, both in not running profits long enough and in allowing losses to run too long. So, you end up with a self-fulfilling prophecy of steady decline until major loss. How do you break the cycle of losses? By simply going back to basics and apply what you have learnt in the markets and refuse to be panicked by short term variations. Do you have the stomach for it?

It has been suggested that the best investors are like top athletes[27]. Perhaps that is exaggerating the situation somewhat, but there are definite similarities: the need for (in the case of professionals) rapid but accurate decision making, the ability to control the adrenaline flow, the ability to concentrate intensely on the subject at hand etc. Ultimately, being close to the edge, the one trade away from a large loss, is of course stressful and exhausting. You and I don't need to be like that but we can give it a go, just to get an appreciation of the pressures on individuals, and perhaps to pick up a little money in the process.

15. THE PARTY MAY LAST LONGER THAN YOU EXPECT

Of course you need to be careful, but applying the "Yin and Yang" concept of stock market investing, in point 8 (Don't chase the market), we noted that chasing the market was not such a clever thing to do, here is almost the opposite idea, if everybody is piling into the FTSE (or dumping it), why not join the party? The last man standing loses! Just make sure it's not you. Certainly, I have often been surprised as to how long a bull run or a bear run lasts and it's a situation that I need to take advantage of more. In fact I tend to get both into and out of a position too early. My tendency also goes against the recommendation of "running your profits". However, it is often difficult to know how long a bull run lasts as the market tends to stop and pause or even go backwards at intervals. That could be because the current run has genuinely ended. Often, though, after a pause "for breath" the market takes off again. Under these conditions it is like trying to get on board a moving train. There seems to me no good time as the technical analysis is only partially helpful in trending situations. Unfortunately, I also have the tendency under these conditions to conclude that the pause for breath is actually an indication of a reversal, but I am wrong too many times!

16. FEAR AND GREED

It is often said that the market is a balance between the two emotions of fear and greed[28]. When you have a profitable position, there is a tendency to be greedy and want more profit, which can sometimes backfire. Sometimes your fear of losing the profit you do have, encourages you to close the position too early. This tends to be my situation: I'm rarely all that greedy, or perhaps I am just more risk averse! Sometimes I'm caught up in the situation and trade in the same direction when a particular rally has already been continuing for a while (see point 15: The party may last longer than you expect). Under these conditions it is often best not to trade at all but simply wait for the next opportunity (see point 8: Don't chase the market). There is a similar fear: the fear of missing out, which even has its own acronym: fomo[29]. In modern society, fomo has become a psychological problem which is much more generic than simply trading on the financial markets. For example, some people incessantly check their phones for messages that may not arrive. With fomo, you see the market moving and want to get in quickly to join the party. I know that I have experienced this quite often. Obviously for successful trading, these emotions need to be tamed. They will perhaps never be eliminated, but you can at least limit your stress by reducing the fear and greed elements. You can certainly reduce the fear by closing positions and you can reduce fomo by walking away from the computer. I don't generally suffer from greed so I can't comment on that element as much, but avoiding entering a trade well after a rally has begun will help. I know that closing positions early is wrong, but if you have a significant profit on the trade and over the long term, is that really so wrong? There is even a stock market saying to support this philosophy (It's never wrong to take a profit).

17. IT IS ONLY MONEY

Remember however you get on, that it is only money! You still have your health and the love of your family and friends! That is, unless your trading has given you heart failure from the frequent adrenaline rush! Money is useful in that you can buy things with it, but it isn't always worth bothering with that much, at least if you are already comfortable. Nobody likes losing it, but your ego is not being tested, just your trading skills. If you need better perspective than that, you can get it here[30].

For the "Yin and Yang" aspect of the comment, I say: Yes, but it is *money!* Basically, there is no point in throwing it away. When you sign up for spread betting companies they recommend that you "bet only with money that you can afford to lose". In some ways, though, this conveys the wrong impression. If you are betting with only money that you can afford to lose, then there is a strong chance that you will go and do just that: lose it! There is a similar daft idea I hear regularly amongst investors and people who make other bets. The argument is that you put in a slug of money, say £1000, and then suppose you make £1000. Then you're in the market for nothing and so you can do anything you like with the profit and you'll still have the initial sum. Of course this is true, but you still need to take care. Otherwise, the £1000 profit will just disappear and you'll be back to scratch. To avoid losing the profit of course, you should treat it in exactly the same way as the initial sum, hopefully with due care and loving attention.

You can apply the same principle to individual trades. It is easy once your trade is showing a profit just to let it run until it exhausts itself to death and you are then left barely breaking even. I've done that a few times and it makes me angry with myself! So, in principle, when you have a buy running, if the conditions are such that, regardless of the position still running, a sell would be your decision, then close the position. The opposite argument holds if you have a short running. This would be a way of protecting your profits, at least to a degree.

5.3 Summary and a mantra

This chapter has discussed a number of contradictory remarks and ideas in common use. Unlike technical analysis, the sayings are too vague and contradictory to be of much practical use. So, make of them what you will. The main thing is to establish your own code of conduct (mantra) and follow it as far as you are able. You are (presumably) human. You will make mistakes, you will break your rules, you will get angry with yourself, you will repeat the same mistakes over and over.... Get over it and get a life. If you make money that's good, but it really doesn't matter. Just enjoy it!

Just as a starting point, here is a brief mantra that I try to follow (not usually all that successfully!):

Think before trading.
Cut losses early.
Run with profits.
Trade in the daytime when the variance is high enough.
Don't chase after opportunities.
Find the current trend and trade with it.
Close positions at the end of the day.
Try to relax: it's only money.

Investing by Spread Betting, by John Austin

6. Options Trading

6.1 Introduction

Rather than spread betting, an alternative way of using leverage is through options trading. With options, you buy (or sell) the right to buy or sell a stock or index at a prefixed price up to a certain date in the future. The leverage arises from the choice of the prefixed price, which can be close to the current price or even far away. Buying an option means that you have the right to the trade at the price indicated, but not the obligation. In other words, if the price goes against you then you can simply let the option expire. Although options give you the right to buy or sell the underlying financial instrument, usually they are traded in their own right, and if they were allowed to expire, their cash value would be returned to the holder.

For example, if a stock is currently priced at £5 per share you might want to buy the right to purchase the share some time in the future at, say, £5.50. Because the buying price is higher than the current price this option would be available quite cheaply, say 25p. All options have an expiration date. If your option has 12 months to run, then it might be reasonable to expect the share price to rise significantly. Suppose, then, that the share price reaches £6 by the expiration date. Then you can exercise your option. You effectively buy the share at £5.50, sell it for £6 and make 50p gain less the 25p cost of purchasing the option, giving a profit of 25p. In practice, rather than exercising the option and selling the share, you simply sell the option. Ordinarily, you would have bought say 1000 options, giving a profit of £250, less any costs. However, suppose instead that the share price crashed to £4 where it stayed until the expiration period of the contract. Then exercising the option would lead to a loss, so you then let the option expire. Despite the share price crashing badly, your only expense has been £250 for the options contract in the first place.

Now compare the situation with spread betting. The equivalent 1000 shares is £10 per point. In the first example the profit is £500 for a gain of 50p, less market spread and interest payments, for a net £450. In the second example, the 100p drop in the share price results in a net £1000 loss plus £50 dealing costs. With options trading, although the potential gain is smaller, the maximum loss is much reduced. Each of these strategies has their advantage and knowledge of them will provide additional trading opportunities, if you care to consider them. On balance, I personally prefer spread betting because the much reduced trading cost allows more frequent trading. Nonetheless, for those interested readers, here is a brief outline of options trading methods. Further details can be found elsewhere, e.g.[31]. First, however, I introduce some jargon, which is even more extreme than spread betting. You quickly get use to it when you trade regularly, so don't be put off by it!

6.2 Some Jargon

Option: The right to trade in an underlying financial instrument at a preset price up to a specific date.

Call Option: The right to buy an underlying financial instrument at an agreed price.

Put Option: The right to to sell an underlying financial instrument at an agreed price.

Strike Price: The price at which the financial instrument is bought or sold.

Expiration Date: The date on which the option expires.

Contract: An option relating to (typically) 100 shares in a stock or 1 point in an index such as the FTSE or Dow.

In the Money: If the option has a net value if traded at the current time it is said to be "in the money".

Out of the Money: If trading the option would result in a cost to the holder, then the option is "out of the money".

Intrinsic value: The amount by which the option is in the money. This is negative if the option is out of the money.

Time value: The price of an option less its intrinsic value.

6.3 Choice of Expiration Date

It is important to consider the expiration date very carefully. The longer the expiration date, the more expensive it is to purchase the option, but the longer you have for your trade to become profitable. Your choice of expiration date depends on your opinion regarding how quickly you can make money versus your appetite for risk. Short-dated options are riskier than ong-dated options, but are cheaper so could end up being more profitable. However, short-dated options may have a risk profile similar to spread betting trades. You could decide on a strategy of using long-dated call options and use the philosophy that everything eventually goes up! This can be effective for indices such as the FTSE or Dow. In the USA, I could purchase options on the Dow with an expiration date of over a year away, although in Britain, IG only provides options for a few months ahead. A reasonable strategy, for example, might be to wait for the Dow to crash, say sometime in the summer when the market is traditionally sold down, and then buy a call option for the end of the calendar year or later. The "Santa Claus" effect, which often leads to a rise in the market towards the end of the year, can then be exploited by selling your call option. However, I have never actually done this. Something always seems to get in the way of what seems like a good investment strategy.

I'm not generally enamoured with put options, except possibly to hedge the value of other items in your portfolio. For example, if you have a portfolio of shares tracking say the FTSE near enough, you might want to buy a put option in case the market crashes. That way you make money on the option to pay for your loss in the main market. It is an expensive way of buying security, though. Generally, you can expect the market to go up, so call options may be more useful over longer time scales.

6.4 Choice of Strike Price

Again the choice of strike price depends on your appetite for risk and your ability to judge how quickly and how far a stock or index price will move. As an example, suppose an option has several months before expiry, and the underlying share is currently trading at £5. You buy a call option at £5, which say costs £1. The share price moves to £6 and it is still prior to the expiration date, so the call option is, for example, now quoted at £1.50 to buy and £1.40 to sell. You go ahead and sell your call option, making £1.40 from the trade giving a profit of 40p. This gives a nice profit of £400 if you've bought 10 contracts. Your outlay was £1000 and profit £400.

Now suppose instead you had bought call options with a strike price of £4, which cost say £2. for the £1000 outlay, you would have only managed to buy 5 contracts. Now with the share price at £6, the £4 strike price would be selling at say £2.40 so that the 5 contracts would net £1200 for a profit of £200.

Of course if the stock price goes down, then the £5 options might be out of the money, and eventually expire worthless. You then lose £1000. Suppose instead you have bought the £4 options and you hang on for dear life hoping that things will turn around. The stock price drops to, say, £4.50 by the expiration date and you get 50p per share or £250 back, a loss of £750. Not as bad as the £5 options, clearly.

So, in summary for a call option, a higher strike price increases the risk and reward. For a put option, a lower strike price increases the risk and reward. When I traded options, I tended to choose the strike price near the current market price. However, after the 2007 financial market crash, options pricing suddenly became more expensive and I never returned to them.

6.5 Options Pricing

There are two components to the value of an option. There is the intrinsic price (which could be negative): the value the option would have if it expired now. The second component is the time value, an additional amount to take into account the time to expiry of the option. Adding the two together gives the total price.

Options have been traditionally priced using the Black-Scholes formula[32], which essentially takes into account market volatility in calculating the price. The way that the stock market moves is modelled on a normal distribution curve with future volatility an unknown in the system of equations. The mathematical details are unnecessary for our discussion here, but can be found in [32]. The way forwards is, rather than calculate the value of an option yourself, assume that the "efficient market" hypothesis[33], the idea that the market has priced everything correctly according to all the knowns in the system, is operating. It is reasonable to suppose that there might be individuals scouring the options prices to find anomalies to trade for their advantage. Once such trades are made, prices would re-establish a new equilibrium with any significant anomaly eliminated.

I suppose, though, it is always worth keeping your eyes open for anomalies. For example, suppose an option with a strike price of x_1 is priced at p_1, while the option for strike price x_2 is priced at p_2. Then you will find that $p_1 - p_2 < x_1 - x_2$, and the difference represents the time value. If you find that in the tables of options prices this inequality no longer occurs, or the succession of price differences $p_1 - p_2$ is not smoothly varying, then you have found an anomaly worthy of further investigation.

Market	Period	Sell	Buy	Change	% Chg	Update	High	Low
FTSE 6625 CALL	MAR-16	320.0	328.0	6611.0	-1.12	17:58:02	349.5	271.2
FTSE 6625 PUT	MAR-16	234.0	242.0	6611.0	-1.12	17:58:02	280.0	221.0
FTSE 6650 CALL	MAR-16	304.4	312.4	6611.0	-1.12	17:58:02	333.4	256.8
FTSE 6650 PUT	MAR-16	243.4	251.4	6611.0	-1.12	17:58:02	290.3	229.9
FTSE 6675 CALL	MAR-16	289.0	297.0	6611.0	-1.12	17:58:02	317.6	243.1
FTSE 6675 PUT	MAR-16	253.0	261.0	6611.0	-1.12	17:58:02	301.0	239.1
FTSE 6600 CALL	MAR-16	274.0	282.0	6611.0	-1.12	17:58:02	302.2	229.8
FTSE 6600 PUT	MAR-16	263.0	271.0	6611.0	-1.12	17:58:02	312.1	248.6
FTSE 6625 CALL	MAR-16	258.6	267.6	6611.0	-1.12	17:58:02	287.1	216.8
FTSE 6625 PUT	MAR-16	273.8	281.8	6611.0	-1.12	17:58:02	323.5	258.9
FTSE 6650 CALL	MAR-16	245.8	253.8	6611.0	-1.12	17:58:02	272.7	204.2
FTSE 6650 PUT	MAR-16	284.8	292.8	6611.0	-1.12	17:58:02	335.5	269.6
FTSE 6675 CALL	MAR-16	232.3	240.3	6611.0	-1.12	17:58:02	258.7	192.0

Example of March 2016 options prices for the FTSE100, from IG markets.

Investing by Spread Betting, by John Austin

I suspect, though, that there may be extended periods of time when the efficient market is not working for options. For example, after the crash of the markets in 2007-2008, the time value of options on the Dow became quite high in my view, indicating that high volatility was being priced in. This is akin to closing the stable door after the horse has bolted. As usual with the stock market, *caveat emptor*!

The Figure above is an example of options pricing as presented by IG markets. Options are offered with strike prices differing by intervals of 25 points, and both calls and puts are presented in this table for strike prices between 6525 and 6675. At this time the FTSE was at about 6735, so all of the calls are in the money. Other tables also exist for strike prices covering a different range. For example, I could buy the 6675 call, which would cost about £240 to buy, although the minimum is 2 contracts. I could buy and then sit and wait. If I were to wait until the expiration date, to make money, the FTSE would need to rise to 6675 + 240 = 6915. Alternately, I could buy the 6650 call which costs about £254 which would require the market to get to 6904 to make money. As the strike price reduces, the price at which the trade is profitable becomes lower, but the options contract is more expensive. I could instead buy the 6525 call at a price of £328, which if I held until option expiration would require the FTSE to exceed 6525 +328 = 6853. The Black-Scholes and other pricing models make the assumption that the time value of the option approaches zero as the time left approaches zero. So, in the final day, the option tends towards the underlying security itself less the strike price. Generally it's best to close your options well before the expiration date, otherwise you would be better off trading with spread bets at lower cost.

The practicalities of trading in options, then, include choice of strike price and expiration date. This means that prices are presented as a table of values which are usually dependent on each other via Black-Scholes or other market models. This requires some practice to understand the different variables and to learn how to trade effectively.

6.6 Level 2 data

Level 2 data on the stock market is essentially the order book: seeing the list of buys and sells that have not yet been exercised. If I want to sell my options at a certain price, this would be higher than the current market price (otherwise I would have an instant trade). Similarly, if I wanted to buy I would specify the highest price that I would be prepared to pay (lower than the market price). Level 2 data puts all this information from all traders together in a table. If you don't have access to Level 2 data, you just see a single buy and sell price. The buy price you see is the *lowest* price that someone is prepared to *sell* at. The sell price you see is the *highest* buy price that somebody else is prepared to pay. Generally, I haven't found Level 2 to be useful information. However, when you trade in options, the market spread can be quite large and this can have a big effect on your profit. So, it is useful to see the order book and then be a little cheeky, especially if you are dealing in small quantities. For example if an option is trading at £1.00 to sell and £1.10 to buy, you might look at the level 2 data and see if you can squeeze out £1.05 to sell. You would put your limit sell price at £1.05 and wait to see if you get any takers. In the example of the choice of strike price in Chapter 6.4, an extra 5p on the options price would change the profit from £400 to £450, a worthwhile gain.

6.7 Summary

As noted in the Introduction to this chapter, I no longer trade options. The main problem with them is their large market spread. Although it can be convenient to buy options to lower the risk, there are other ways of lowering risk with spread betting, primarily by staying in cash for most of the time. The advantage of options, however, is that you can take the longer term view and not have to worry about your positions as much. For some people, options may be better: the choice is yours!

Investing by Spread Betting, by John Austin

7. Trading Diary

7.1 Introduction

It is often suggested by spread betting companies that a trading diary could be beneficial in increasing your profits. Don't forget that the spread betting company has your interests at heart because you are essentially working for the company generating its profits. I would agree that a trading diary is useful and although I didn't keep one through the first three months of my recent trading with IG, I carried out a postmortem of all my trades to see what I was doing wrong. This enabled me to correct certain mistakes, establish what works for me and perhaps accept that I will continue to make certain "errors" because of the sort of person I am. In particular I am punctual, so I usually arrive early at a party but, apparently drunk on my paper profits, seem to prefer to leave early as well. The conclusions I have come to in this book of course are a distillation of the learning process, not just in my period of IG trading but during the many years prior to that as well using leveraged products. Consequently, much of the TA material is well known to me, even if I seem at times to lack the skills to exploit it in practice. The TA always seems obvious in hindsight but because TA only tells what has happened it has limited predictive skills. Misinterpretation of the TA message, then is often a source of losses.

During the early stages of my recent trading with IG, I was trading about 10-12 times per day, and the details of this period would be too lengthy to include here. Instead, I here include my trading diary for July and August 2015, and my daily win/loss record for the period April to August. One of the things that will become apparent is how stupid I am at times. You can't possibly be as daft as that! So, if I can make a profit, you can make a bigger one. These details together with up to date figures and commentary are included on my website[34].

7.2 Monthly Account Summaries

March 2015

I began with a sum of £300, which was all I had immediately available from my bank account, and I started trading with IG markets. I traded mostly the £/$ exchange rate but also the Dow and the FTSE100. I tried to use "technical analysis", concentrating on MACD and momentum as well as using the Bollinger bands. Within a week, I had lost half my original sum and so I decided to wait a few days to transfer more funds from a share sale! After further losses, I had almost recouped all my earlier sum by the end of the month.

Total Gain for the Month = -£54.73

Here are my daily profits and losses for the month.

Date	Total Sum	Daily Profit	Monthly profit
11/03/15	£271.40	-£28.60	-£28.60
12/03/15	£401.23	£129.83	£101.23
13/03/15	£169.93	-£231.30	-£130.07
20/03/15	£1,125.53	-£44.40	-£174.47
23/03/15	£1,136.73	£11.16	-£163.27
24/03/15	£1,040.03	-£96.70	-£253.97
25/03/15	£1,084.87	£44.84	-£215.13
26/03/15	£1,227.92	£143.05	-£72.08
27/03/15	£1,282.67	£54.75	-£17.33
30/03/15	£1,218.07	-£64.60	-£81.93
31/03/15	£1,245.27	£27.20	-£54.73

April 2015

Already £55 down the tubes, I was hoping for better in April. After a long campaign, trading typically 10 times per day and spending most of my time glued to my computer, I finally emerged with a net £10 overall profit at the end of the month (and £65 for April itself). In late April my account was even down almost £200 but recovered completely the next day. Having actually made money by the end of the month, it was tempting to think that I had finally understood this trading game, but as it turned out, I still had a lot to learn!

Total Gain for the Month = £64.90

Here are my daily profits and losses for the month.

Date	Total Sum	Daily Profit	Monthly profit
01/04/15	£1,266.97	£21.70	£21.70
02/04/15	£1,211.17	-£55.80	-£34.10
03/04/15	£1,196.37	-£14.80	-£48.90
06/04/15	£1,225.47	£29.10	-£19.80
07/04/15	£1,224.37	-£1.10	-£20.90
08/04/15	£1,246.47	£22.10	£1.20
09/04/15	£1,224.47	-£22.00	-£20.80
10/04/15	£1,203.77	-£20.70	-£41.50
13/04/15	£1,175.54	-£28.23	-£69.73
14/04/15	£1,229.04	£53.50	-£16.23
15/04/15	£1,189.24	-£39.80	-£56.03
16/04/15	£1,243.94	£54.70	-£1.33
17/04/15	£1,269.04	£25.10	£23.77
20/04/15	£1,208.94	-£60.10	-£36.33
21/04/15	£1,101.54	-£107.40	-£143.73
22/04/15	£1,305.54	£204.00	£60.27
23/04/15	£1,249.17	-£56.37	£3.90
24/04/15	£1,268.37	£19.20	£23.10
27/04/15	£1,320.57	£52.20	£75.30

28/04/15	£1,329.57	£9.00	£84.30
29/04/15	£1,250.17	-£79.40	£4.90
30/04/15	£1,310.17	£60.00	£64.90

May 2015

The month began with the account back in the black. The profit then built up, reaching a healthy £176 on 18th May. Thereafter it started to go downhill and I ended up the month over £50 down. The cause of the loss wasn't apparent at this stage, so I continued with my investment strategy, with frequent trading on the FTSE100.

Total Gain for the Month = -£51.80

Here are my daily profits and losses for the month.

Date	Total Sum	Daily Profit	Monthly profit
01/05/15	£1,302.17	-£8.00	-£8.00
05/05/15	£1,293.37	-£8.80	-£16.80
06/05/15	£1,340.57	£47.20	£30.40
07/05/15	£1,322.77	-£17.80	£12.60
08/05/15	£1,446.17	£123.40	£136.00
11/05/15	£1,391.57	-£54.60	£81.40
12/05/15	£1,430.37	£38.80	£120.20
13/05/15	£1,357.37	-£73.00	£47.20
14/05/15	£1,402.37	£45.00	£92.20
15/05/15	£1,436.97	£34.60	£126.80
18/05/15	£1,486.97	£50.00	£176.80
19/05/15	£1,408.97	-£78.00	£98.80
20/05/15	£1,404.97	-£4.00	£94.80
21/05/15	£1,401.37	-£3.60	£91.20
22/05/15	£1,390.47	-£10.90	£80.30
25/05/15	£1,394.17	£3.70	£84.00
26/05/15	£1,338.17	-£56.00	£28.00
27/05/15	£1,248.57	-£89.60	-£61.60

28/05/15	£1,212.97	-£35.60	-£97.20
29/05/15	£1,258.37	£45.40	-£51.80

June 2015

        The month began £40 down from my original sum in March and after a few days of gains became steadily worse. By the 18th June, the account was over £300 in the red, and almost £280 for the month. From here, a change of strategy was needed.

        Up until now, I had traded on a short timescale expecting to close my position in half an hour or less. This usually worked effectively while the market volume was high enough that the technical analysis was reasonably reliable. However, I often realised that I was closing a position at a loss only to find the market turn around. If I had only kept my positions open for a much longer time then most of the losses would have given profits. Accordingly, towards the end of June I reduced the trading frequency from typically 10 trades per day to more like 3 or less. Profits returned, and I ended up the month at break even. Not particularly good for a month's work, but better than a kick in the pants!

Total Gain for the Month = -£0.67

Here are my daily profits and losses for the month.

Date	Total Sum	Daily Profit	Monthly profit
01/06/15	£1,308.57	£50.20	£50.20
02/06/15	£1,366.87	£58.30	£108.50
03/06/15	£1,319.47	-£47.40	£61.10
04/06/15	£1,227.14	-£92.33	-£31.33
05/06/15	£1,175.14	-£52.00	-£83.33
08/06/15	£1,134.54	-£40.60	-£123.93
09/06/15	£1,095.94	-£38.60	-£162.53
10/06/15	£1,072.34	-£23.60	-£186.13
11/06/15	£1,117.34	£45.00	-£141.13

12/06/15	£1,123.14	£5.80	-£135.33
15/06/15	£1,095.54	-£27.60	-£162.93
16/06/15	£1,098.14	£2.60	-£160.33
17/06/15	£979.34	-£118.80	-£279.13
18/06/15	£1,084.03	£104.69	-£174.44
19/06/15	£1,042.32	-£41.71	-£216.15
22/06/15	£1,162.02	£119.70	-£96.45
23/06/15	£1,163.32	£1.30	-£95.15
24/06/15	£1,135.92	-£27.40	-£122.55
25/06/15	£1,177.38	£41.46	-£81.09
26/06/15	£1,309.18	£131.80	£50.71
29/06/15	£1,350.18	£41.00	£91.71
30/06/15	£1,257.70	-£92.48	-£0.67

July 2015

I suppose there is always some excuse, but this month political uncertainty over Greek debts contributed to swings in the market which I was able to trade successfully. Profits peaked in the middle of the month at over £750 but thereafter declined steadily and my confidence started to wane. In the last few days of the month I managed to stop the rot, and started to make progress again, but the account is still almost £200 short of its highest.

Total Gain for the Month = £573.37

Here are my daily profits and losses for the month.

Date	Total Sum	Daily Profit	Monthly profit
01/07/15	£1,395.10	£137.40	£137.40
02/07/15	£1,431.50	£36.40	£173.80
03/07/15	£1,448.50	£17.00	£190.80
05/07/15	£1,509.10	£60.60	£251.40
06/07/15	£1,604.70	£95.60	£347.00
07/07/15	£1,645.50	£40.80	£387.80
08/07/15	£1,659.83	£14.33	£402.11

09/07/15	£1,912.75	£252.92	£655.05
10/07/15	£1,895.75	-£17.00	£638.05
13/07/15	£1,919.35	£23.60	£661.65
14/07/15	£1,905.01	-£14.34	£647.31
15/07/15	£2,012.01	£107.00	£754.31
16/07/15	£1,909.47	-£102.54	£651.77
17/07/15	£1,862.47	-£47.00	£604.77
20/07/15	£1,823.47	-£39.00	£565.77
21/07/15	£1,877.73	£54.26	£620.03
22/07/15	£1,813.93	-£63.80	£556.23
23/07/15	£1,828.53	£14.60	£570.83
24/07/15	£1,754.43	-£74.10	£496.73
27/07/15	£1,792.79	£38.36	£535.09
28/07/15	£1,744.07	-£48.72	£486.37
29/07/15	£1,753.27	£9.20	£495.57
30/07/15	£1,810.27	£57.00	£552.57
31/07/15	£1,831.07	£20.80	£573.37

August 2015

This month there was more turmoil on the markets due to the instability of the Chinese financial markets. As usual, it seems to have been overdone, but I wasn't able to exploit the situation, losing a lot of money in volatile markets. I paid the price for trading the Chinese market with one trade costing me over £300 in less than 10 minutes. If it weren't for that trade, August would have come out only slightly down. I vow to keep it simple in the future!

Total Gain for the Month = -£360.92

Here are my daily profits and losses for the month.

Date	Total sum	Profit	Daily Profit	Monthly Profit
03/08/15	£1,877.27	£577.27	£46.20	£46.20
04/08/15	£1,908.87	£608.87	£31.60	£77.80
05/08/15	£1,809.47	£509.47	-£99.40	-£21.60
06/08/15	£1,820.36	£520.36	£10.89	-£10.71
07/08/15	£1,842.85	£542.85	£22.49	£11.78
10/08/15	£1,842.85	£542.85	£0.00	£11.78
11/08/15	£1,871.35	£571.35	£28.50	£40.28
12/08/15	£1,872.25	£572.25	£0.90	£41.18
13/08/15	£1,854.25	£554.25	-£18.00	£23.18
14/08/15	£1,858.25	£558.25	£4.00	£27.18
17/08/15	£1,977.15	£677.15	£118.90	£146.08
18/08/15	£1,662.65	£362.65	-£314.50	-£168.42
19/08/15	£1,701.25	£401.25	£38.60	-£129.82
20/08/15	£1,677.65	£377.65	-£23.60	-£153.42
21/08/15	£1,747.65	£447.65	£70.00	-£83.42
24/08/15	£1,661.65	£361.65	-£86.00	-£169.42
25/08/15	£1,703.05	£403.05	£41.40	-£128.02
26/08/15	£1,521.15	£221.15	-£181.90	-£309.92
27/08/15	£1,522.95	£222.95	£1.80	-£308.12
28/08/15	£1,522.95	£222.95	£0.00	-£308.12
31/08/15	£1,470.15	£170.15	-£52.80	-£360.92

7.3 Trading Diary July 2015

30/6/15: At 7.00 am I opened a FTSE long at 6571 and closed at 6588, shortly after the market officially opened at 8.05 am, for a nice chunky profit of £34. The market continued to go up, so I opened another long at 11.10 am at 6602. Due to the situation in Greece, the market completely tanked, leaving me nursing a loss on the trade of over £125, but the long term trend seemed up, so I left my position open for the rest of the day.

1/7/15: Yesterday's position turned around and I was able to close at the end of the trading day at 6608 for a small profit of £12.

2/7/15:I went long again on the FTSE at 7.00 am at 6583.6 and picked up 25.2 points for a profit of £50.40 at 9.05 am. The market continued to rise during the day. The technical analysis in late afternoon suggested a reduction was on the cards, so I went short twice but lost money: the first time a loss of £15 the second time a gain of £1.

3/7/15:I made several small trades netting a gain for the day of £17.

5/7/15: The situation in Greece still had not stabilised, so as information came out during the weekend, the "Sunday FTSE" market was worth trading, despite the 20 pt spread. The previous Friday's market suggested that 6450 was a lower limit for the FTSE with bad news. The Sunday FTSE was on offer at 6462 by 11pm, so I went long as the news was improving. By midnight it had already reached 6500 and rather than risk a nice chunky profit, I took my profits and went to bed!

6/7/15: With the FTSE getting a bit difficult to predict because of the political situation, I tried the S & P 500, going long at £10/pt at 6.49 am, closing an hour later for a £44 profit. finally, I managed to work out what was going on with the FTSE, and I shorted it at 3.53 pm at 6558 closing at 6540 for a nice chunky profit of £36. I also picked up another £16 in the evening going long at 6510 at 8.04 pm closing at 6518 at 8.22 pm.

7/7/15:I made 2 long trades one in the morning and one in the afternoon, and managed to pick up £20 each time, for a gain on the day of £41.

8/7/15: Not a very satisfactory day as my morning trade was cancelled out by my lunchtime trade. I know I shouldn't trade at lunchtime..... I managed to pick up a few pounds in the evening, but I should have let my short run into the evening and then I would have picked up another £40. The political situation was developing, and the market was quite low, so I went long at 6465 at 9.10 pm. I thought it would go to 6500 but get stuck there, so I put a limit sell at 6495. Then I went to bed! I woke up at 4am to go to the bathroom (!) and I just could not resist checking my position. It had already closed with the £60 profit in the bag, so I went back to bed content. Alas, my contentment did not last long as the market continued well past 6500 the next day!

9/7/15:I couldn't understand why the market had got so high, so I thought a downward correction was due soon. In the afternoon I tried shorting the FTSE twice, picking up £18 on each occasion. Timing wan't great, I could have easily have got £30 both times, but a profit is a profit. The market did eventually drop but not by a huge amount. There was still some political risk, but I thought that the EU would eventually help out Greece. By 8 pm the market looked as if it had bottomed out, so I put in a buy order at 6552. This was picked up at 8.30 pm while I was watching Netflix. I thought that 6600 would be a reasonable limit, but I didn't want to add one this time as it cost me to do so previously. By 11 pm Greece had submitted its austerity plan as promised and the market went out of control. I looked at my position and by 11.20 pm there was £190 profit. You just can't turn that away, so I closed at 6645 for a profit of £185.

10/7/15:I had a go, but after the profits of the week, my heart wasn't in it and I went back to my bad habits closing two positions for small profits (£11 combined) and a loss of £29. I'm sort of annoyed with myself, because if my short from 6675 was kept running I could have closed for a large profit. I was confused about the time that the IG markets DFB FTSE was open for..... Investing is all about what could have happened and one needs to bury the frustrations of the past and approach each new day with a fresh perspective.

13/7/15:I didn't know what to do this morning because of the continuing political uncertainty. There was a surge of over 100 pts in the FTSE just before 8 am, but I missed it completely as I was having breakfast! I looked at BBC news but the Greece situation was still not completely resolved. So I thought the rise was overdue and I tried shorting the market. Unfortunately I took too long over making my decisions and made two trades in short succession going short at 6731.5 for £9.60 profit and 6727.5 for £13 profit. But I closed far too early; the market continued to drop and I made the fatal mistake of shorting again at 6715.5. After picking up a few pounds, the market reversed and at one stage the trade was almost £50 down. It turned around again and eventually I closed at near enough break even (£1 profit). What a mess, but £23 up on the trades at least! For the rest of the day, the FTSE settled around the 6730 level and there were no opportunities to trade.

14/7/15: There may be a downward correction to the FTSE today, although the current overall upward trend may well continue for a few days. So it's a matter of looking for opportunities in either direction and trade for the short term until a clear signal emerges. IG have increased their overnight FTSE spread from 5 to 7 pts, so there is no point in trading before 7.00 am when the European market opens and the spread drops to 2 pts. After a typical surge upwards at 7.00 am, the surge looked as if it was running out of steam, so I opened a short at 6738.3. within a few minutes I was in profit and the price returned to the moving average. I closed at about 7.10 am for a £9 profit, but I should have held on as the market continued to go down. The market looked as if it had settled, so I went long at 6725.5. My timing wasn't great and I went to an immediate loss but it turned around and then just after 8.00 am it went up. At one stage my profit was over £20, but instead of closing, I let the position continue and closed for a gain of just £1. I needed to have hung on another 10 minutes. the same happened later in the morning; I went long at 6714.5 after the selling seemed to die out, but it took a long time for significant profit. I gave up in the end for a £1 profit. during the afternoon the FTSE rose slowly, which was annoying. It seemed to get stuck at around 6750, so I chose to go short at 6746.8 at about 3.30 pm. Unfortunately, after an initial reduction, the price continued to rise. At one point my position was £24 down. I am letting it run; I just don't believe that a correction is not due at some time, particularly as the Greek situation is not fully resolved. At the time of writing (5.20 pm) my position is still down by £12. If I have the patience this could go a long way (positive or negative)!

15/7/15: I checked the charts first thing in the morning and discovered that overnight the market had peaked near 6780 so my short would have been over £70 down the tubes, while I slept peacefully. By 6 am the market was moving back in my favour and there was a further downward movement when in turn the European and British markets opened. My position went into profit but the profit was oscillating wildly: the usual froth of early morning trading. Eventually, the market had dropped to 6730 and I thought that that may be the low of the day, so I closed at 6730.8 for a profit of £32 less £0.74 short interest. In the above table, by the way, the loss for 14 July is a bit artificial as it includes the running loss of the short. In turn, today's profit will end up getting exaggerated unless I have another position open overnight.

It seems that my judgement this morning turned out well. Up until the early afternoon, the market went up reaching about 6775. This hardly seems to reflect the political uncertainty. The IMF this morning attacked the Eurozone countries for its lax lending policies to Greece. Yet Greece has already agreed more austerity than its people voted for a few days ago. It is difficult to see how the terms can be accepted by the Greek parliament. In any case, the EU is a sort of socialist organisation for countries whereas of course the IMF comes over as being quite right wing. It doesn't care about the Greek people as long as it gets its money back, and I suppose that's as it should be. But Germany is a bit confused. It seems to want to be part of the European "experiment" but not support the weak countries. That's a contradiction. There is no doubt that the Greeks are hurting. Decades of fraud from their politicians has contributed to the current state. So, if we believe in the EU at all then we must bail out Greece, the non Eurozone countries as well. That must affect our economy. I think the current market surge has therefore been overdone. So just after 12.30 I went short again, this time at 6774.8. It's a bit unusual for me to trade at this time, but I think this is a long term (multi-hour or up to Friday) trade. I have been busy painting my house, so I wasn't able to put these thoughts down at the time of my trade. It is now about 2.15 pm and my position is showing a running profit of about £18. Not a bad start!

The previous political argument notwithstanding, I thought that discretion was the better part of valour and at about 3.30 pm I bailed out for a profit of 25.2 pts/£50.40. This seems to have been the right decision for the moment.

16/7/15: I became more convinced of my previous arguments, so in the evening of the 15th I opened up another short on the FTSE at 6739.4. What was I thinking of? The Greek vote came in favour of the EU deal and the market surged. At one point, my position was down the tubes by over £130. I should have opened a second short from there as the market retreated, but I didn't. Eventually the market settled down with me nursing losses of about £100. I left my position to run and went to bed. It was no different in the morning of the 16th. Once the Euopean market opened, my losses narrowed but at the moment I'm still £70 odd down and contemplating bailing out.

I eventually bailed out at the end of the day for a loss of £101.80, so I have lost almost all my profit for the week. I had several opportunities to bail out earlier at a much better price, at one time for a loss of only £25. It is always so difficult deciding when to bail a losing position, but at least it's done now and I can start fresh tomorrow. I was expecting the multi-day MACD analysis to indicate a peak, but it seems now the peak won't be for a few days. The worst result in weeks!

17/7/15: After increasing from 7 am to 8am in off-market trading, the early froth of the market indicated a downward trend, so I went short on the FTSE at 6794.5. It seems bizarre that after yesterday's fiasco, I'm short again. After 10 minutes or so, the market seemed to be heading back up, so I closed at 6784.5 for a profit of £20. This seemed to be the best decision for a while, but half an hour later the FTSE seemed to be heading down again, but I no longer have a position running. I made several other trades during the day, using technical analysis as a guide but the market seemed to change direction just after I traded each time. In several cases I should have just left my position running but after yesterday's performance, I wanted to keep a tight stop, mentally if not explicitly setting one on the trading platform. I made too many simple mistakes today, such as reacting too quickly to market conditions. The net result was an overall loss for the day of £47 and it has not been a good week, down £33 on the week. hopefully next week will be better!

20/7/15: The multi-day charts suggest overall that the recent rise has peaked, so I started looking for a chance to sell the FTSE. Between 7 and 8am as the European markets started trading, the movement was downward, but I missed the chance to go short. Once the main market opened the FTSE recovered again and showed an increase. however, the surge appeared short-lived, so at about 8.30 am I opened a short at 6787.8. The price has moved a little since then, and at the time of writing the position is showing a £13 profit. The profit built up a little and then reversed. At one stage my position was down by almost £50 so clearly I should have closed. In the morning I tried opening a second short but that was ill advised and I closed with a £15 loss. I left the initial position running and by mid afternoon the FTSE price had turned around again and at one point I was up by almost £30. Again, I should have closed, but I thought that there was more available. I have left the position running overnight, and by 8 pm in the off-market, the trade was showing a loss of £24. I think the multi-day trend will change to down, as the MACD histograms are now decreasing. 6800 or so for the FTSE seems to be an upper limit at the moment.

21/7/15: My FTSE short lost more money overnight and in the market froth just before 7 am I was almost £50 down. Fortunately, the position turned around, and mindful of yesterday's effort I decided to close at near break even for a profit of £4.40 less £0.74 short interest. It didn't take long for me to regret closing, as the market dropped 10 points within 10 minutes, but I will look for a chance to sell again at 6790 or so. A little later the MACD histograms suggested that the market was going up, so I bought at 6773.1. However, as the overall market was still trending down, there was a danger of the price bouncing off the moving average, near 6781. So I closed at 6781.1 for a profit of £16. The market continued to rise and I went short again at 6794.1. Unfortunately, the market stalled and for some reason I became a little anxious, closing at a profit of £10.60. That was a mistake, as the market has subsequently dropped significantly and I could be £70 up on the trade if I had left it running. In the above table, todays profit includes the £30 of trade profits less the running loss of yesterday.

22/7/15: I was already annoyed that I had closed my FTSE short for a small profit prior to its large move down. The loss of the FTSE continued but by about 7.20 am or so the price seemed to stall and go up, so I went long at 6731.8. That was a big mistake as the price first dropped a little then tanked. At one stage I was well over £50 down and again the price seemed to be starting to turn around. rather than close my first position I opened a second long from 6713.1. I closed this relatively quickly for a £13 gain which at least cancelled out some of the losses on the other position. Eventually, I closed my first position for a loss of £32.40 and a loss of £19.40 on the day so far. Not ideal, but at least I was able to rescue a potentially very bad situation. By the afternoon, the FTSE had dropped to around 6700 and then started to recover, so I went long at 6711. This moved in my favour at first and then turned around. While I was not watching, the market tanked, and I was down over £110 at one point. I was able to manage my losses a little, picking up a £21 profit on a quick trade by opening a second long. Eventually, my first position recovered somewhat, but I was still well down by the end of the day. This is not the time to be long on the multi-day time scale, so I closed for a loss of £71 and a total loss for the day of £64, once the dividend was taken into account. I am now £200 down on my peak profit of this time last week, but I live to fight another day!

23/7/15: The FTSE increased overnight but then gradually dropped for much of the day. I went short a few times in the morning picking up a few points, but the movements seemed quite slow and I didn't commit to the sells. I was otherwise occupied in the afternoon, so I didn't trade. This was a pity as some money could have been made. Overall, I came out ahead by £14.60. During the early evening the FTSE continued to drop in the off-market trading and looks to have reached its minimum at about 6627 or so. I have put in a buy order at 6635. The price has gone below the multi-day mean and I believe it is due an upward correction after such a large fall. Only a day or so ago the FTSE had exceeded 6800.

24/7/15: My 6635 FTSE buy order was picked up last night and at one stage I was almost £20 up. By the morning, however, that had evaporated and I was a similar amount in arrears. Just before the European market opened the FTSE started to tick up, and there was another rise at the 8 am official UK market open. As usual, it was volatile over the next 10 minutes and so I decided to take profits at 6647.6 for a profit of £24 after overnight interest. As usual, if I had been a little more patient, 20 min. later I could have had another £10, but it would have been difficult to have stomached the large loss of profit at 8.15 am.

25/7/15: In fact the closure of my long position yesterday was way too early as the market continued up to about 6680, so I could have picked up another £60. Thereafter, the market continued to drop and I thought it prudent to await a buying opportunity. There was more loss towards the end of the day and the FTSE dropped below 6600. I couldn't understand it at all, and so during one of the lulls I bought back in at 6597.5. what was I thinking? I made the cardinal sin of ignoring some of the TA signals. The stock market philosophy is to kick a man when he's down, so the market continued to tank. I was too mystified to close my position, so I am now £98 down on the trade. It looks as if this is now a long-term trade!

27/7/15: This morning the market became completely chaotic but I was too paralysed to take advantage. At one point, my long position (running on from Friday) went to a deficit of only about £20 before the FTSE plunged 50 points. It then surged back up again and by mid-morning had got back to over 6580. It became apparent that this was about the maximum for a while, perhaps for the day, so I closed at 6582.3 for a loss of about £34 including long interest over the weekend. Usually, the market settles down by mid-morning, so once the reduction from the peak occurred I went long again as suggested by the MACD diagnostic, this time at 6570.8. so, I am in exactly the same position as on Friday with a FTSE long running, but at 11.5 points lower. If the stock were an item of clothing in a shop or something, I have "saved £23"! Now that the market has come up significantly from its low of 6540 ish, the MACD analysis for the multi-day timescale may be starting to turn around, so I believe the worst on the downside may be over.

Well, I was quite wrong there. My long position started losing, so I closed for a £25 loss. The FTSE dropped to the 6540 region where it stabilised for a while, so I went long again at 6545. After about half an hour, the market resumed its downward spiral, so I closed for a further loss of £18. The FTSE even dropped below 6500 at one stage in the late afternoon, and fool like I am, I went long again at 6510. In view of my recent poor trades, I closed quickly (too quickly) for a £15 gain. After these recent falls, the multi-day trend has resumed its reduction, but I am still reluctant to "join the party" bashing the FTSE, as it's not clear how much longer this can last.

Net profit for the day was £38, consisting of the closing of Friday's position at a lower loss than on Friday, a few small losses during the day and one small profitable trade. I should have just closed Friday's long and gone short. I'm now entirely in cash.

28/7/15: After overnight gains, the early morning direction in the FTSE was difficult to make out. I made two short trades, one gain one loss, with a net loss of £8. I am now waiting to see whether the market makes any overall move. I made a few small trades during the rest of the day, but I couldn't see any net direction and by the closing of the official market I was at near enough break even. However, by about 5 pm, the off-market continued a rise that looked a bit toppy. So I opened a short at 6566.8. I regretted this straight away, as the market barely moved but come the evening the position rapidly deteriorated.

29/7/15: In the above accounts for the 28th yesterday evening's loss is included as £46. By this morning the loss had reduced to about £35 but oscillating a bit leaving me wondering what to do with this trade -- whether to close soon or leave for a few hours in the prospect of getting a better result.

Investing by Spread Betting, by John Austin

Soon before 8 am, it was clear that I had to close my short. I really left it too late and the loss on the trade in the end was £59. Although the technical analysis did not seem to give clear buy signals, the upward moving trend (100 min. average) and the price staying close to or above the upper Bollinger band suggested an upward movement. I then bought back in at 6594 and the market soared upwards to over 6610. Unfortunately I didn't close, and the market became extremely volatile. I closed at a loss of £10, only to see the market stabilise again, so I bought back in at a slightly lower price (6590.8, having closed at 6588.8). After losing again, I'm near break even for the trade and about £25 down on the day so far. What a mess! With spread betting you can lose money on the way up and lose money on the way down! In principle, the long term trend is now up, at least if the multi-day chart is to be believed.

The FTSE spent most of the day going up and down without any appreciable direction and I made the cardinal sin of closing my trades before giving them chance to work. In several trades, I ended up losing about £20 total but I was angry with myself and finally in the afternoon an opportunity to go long again presented itself. This time, I endured the market fall just before 2 pm and eventually the market soared again to set a new high for the day. I closed a little too early for a profit of £42 and a net £9 up on the day. With the multi-day moving average now at about 6663 I will look for this as a target once an opportunity to go long presents itself again.

30/7/15: Again, there was an overnight increase in the FTSE but I was out of the market. In the morning froth I made a few trades alternately short and long, each trade winning small amounts for a total of £27. The FTSE has slipped back under 6640 and, again I await an opportunity to go long for a longer time scale trade.

I should have gone long when I had the chance, as the market moved up almost 50 points. Then, soon after the US market opened, both the US and UK markets crashed and I went long at 6651.8. I closed early to protect my £27 profit. A little later, I opened a short at 6664.8, but I became ludicrously nervous and closed for a slight gain of £3 for a total of £57 for the day. It wasn't optimal, but not bad by any means. I have made too many little trades today (6), but at least they were all winning.

31/7/15: The early morning FTSE market was relatively quiet. I did make one trade shorting from 6685 to 6678.3 for a profit of £13.40 but in my usual style, I didn't time the close of my position well and I could easily have picked up another 3 or 4 points. The market has now gone up again, so I couldn't have waited all that long. I made several other short trades during the day, not all succesful. In a slow moving market it was difficult to make out the movements, until it was too late. There were opportunities to go long at various times, but I didn't expect the recent high values of the FTSE to hold. In hindsight, the correct strategy looks to have been easy: short until late morning and then go long for the rest of the day. That would have netted about 70 points, but instead I picked up only 10. Anyway, I finished with a profit of £570 for July, less than the peak reached on 9 July, but still fairly healthy.

7.4 Trading Diary August 2015

3/8/15: I made 3 trades in the early morning froth, but my timing was quite poor so I barely broke even. I first went long at 6674 at about 7.15 am and, after the market dipped to below 6670, it took off again. Relieved that my position was back in the black, I closed too early. The market surged to 6690+ which I thought was overdone, and I went short at 6695. Unfortunately, I got hit by a spike which panicked me into closing my position. I should have held on, because the market turned around quickly and the opportunity to short the market arose again. Unfortunately, I didn't time the exit from the 3rd trade very well, so I made a profit of £8, when over £20 was available. The net profit from the 3 trades was a miserly £0.80!

With the FTSE close to the multi-day moving average, overall trends are small as we await a transition up or down. I made some further trades in the morning picking up a few pounds. Then in the early afternoon trading, soon after the opening of the US market, the FTSE plunged back close to what looks like the support line at about 6670. Once I was confident that breach of the support line wasn't likely, I went long at 6674 and was able to ride the FTSE up. I bailed at near enough the right time for once for a pleasing profit on the trade of £28, for a total of £46 profit on the day.

4/8/15: Yesterday evening, the FTSE crashed following the US market. however, the fall looked overdone, so I went long at 6645. Rather than watch the markets all evening, I closed later for a profit of £12. As it happens, there was a second opportunity to go long, at an even lower price, but I was having dinner at the time. By this morning, the market had recovered some of its losses, but it does suggest that perhaps the multi-day trend may switch to negative. I went short at 6675.3 soon after 8 am, and closed 5 or 10 minutes later on what I thought was a downward spike at 6664, for a profit of £22.60. The downward movement actually continued quite a way and at the time of writing (9.04 am) the FTSE is still only 6661, but apparently increasing.

I should have gone long of the FTSE just after 9 am, as after I wrote the above paragraph, it went up 40 pts! I didn't expect the increase to be so large, and by the time I thought about it, the upward trend was running out of steam. I placed one long trade picking up £6 before the FTSE looked as if it was retreating. I then went short at quite a good price (6698.2) at about 9.30 am, but I panicked when the market spiked upwards. I closed for a loss of of £29 on the trade, leaving me to curse my stupidity as the market subsequently dropped over 30 points. From here it was difficult to see any movement and I was left picking up bits and pieces here and there: at least all my little trades were profitable. In the end I finished the day with a profit of £31.60, including yesterday evening's £12.

In the multi-day chart, the MACD histograms are still increasing slowly, so the future movement of the FTSE is still unclear: more likely up than down.

5/8/15: I completely mishandled the opening of the market. Several times, the FTSE looked to be going up, so I went long, consistent with the possibility that the multi-day upwards trend may continue after its recent stabilisation. However, my positions quickly went into the black a few pounds, only to reverse themselves. This happened four times at various prices, so I am nursing a loss of £42 for the morning so far. An upward trend seems now to be established, so I have lost money for nothing. I have gone long again at 6714.9, so we will see if I have messed up again!

 The market tanked soon after I opened my long position, and thinking that a multi-day downward trend was becoming established, I closed my long with another loss of over £40. The FTSE was difficult to make out for much of the day but it did eventually turn around and now indicates an upward trend for the next few days. Unfortunately, I made many trades sometimes up sometimes down losing more money. My logic seemed to have deserted me today and I emerged with a loss of £99 for the day, the worst performance since 16th July. I seem to have done everything wrong today.

6/8/15: The American market tanked just after the UK market closed, and this had an effect on the FTSE off-market. US borrowing requirements were apparently $1 billion worse than expected, but this doesn't seem a big deal to me: the US is always borrowing huge amounts of money. The FTSE also dropped from yesterday's closing price and last night I thought it had stabilised at around 6730. So, I went long at 6733.9. Unfortunately, the market continued to drop overnight. At one time this morning, soon after the opening of the European markets, my position was £57 down. It has recovered significantly and a couple of times it nudged positive. However, I thought the longer term trend was still positive, so I didn't close. that may have been a mistake, as my position is now over £25 down.

My FTSE long recovered nicely, rising to over 6760, which would have been a profit of over £50. Unfortunately, I was away from home at the time, and didn't close my position. I was wondering whether to set a limit at 6760 as well.... When I got home, at about 2.30 pm, my profit was around £30 and started decreasing fast! It looked grim, and I procrastinated, eventually closing at a mere £6.60 profit. Then of course, the FTSE reversed, leaving me cursing. I made a few small trades in the afternoon, but I only picked up a few scraps. Profit for the day was £12 less long interest. Although the FTSE didn't move much overall today, the multi-day trend is still up and perhaps if I do get a good price overnight, I might try repeating the experience (preferably less the bit where I have a large paper loss and close at a decent profit).

7/8/15: Yesterday evening, I placed a long order on the FTSE at 6735, and it was picked up while I was watching Netflix. I looked at my position from time to time, and it was going in the right direction. By 11 pm, it had reached a gain of £25. I don't usually like to risk overnight positions, so I closed there. By the morning prices were up very slightly, by a couple of points, but starting to go down. Unfortunately, I didn't take that as a hint, and went long at near enough the same price as I closed last night. My position moved away from me, but at one time I could have closed at almost break even. Thinking there was more on the table, I ended up closing with a £17 loss. I did one trade in the 8 am froth, going short, but my opening price was too high and I only picked up a point. With the early morning losses, the MACD histogram trend may be about to reverse. I'm guessing that with this uncertainty, today may be a quiet day with no overall direction. It may be a good day for picking up scraps: 3 or 4 points from time to time.

As I suspected, the FTSE was quiet most of the day and I only made one more trade, going long just after 2.30 pm when the market looked to be about to turn around. I picked up £13 within about 10 minutes and left it there for the day. In retrospect the best trade would have been to have gone short just after mid-day, but that wasn't clear at the time. Net profit for the day was £22, enough to wipe out my bad result from Wednesday. With the FTSE having fallen overall during the day, its future trend now seems unclear. Losses on the US market will probably have a negative effect on the FTSE for a little while yet, so the FTSE may start to tick down.

10/8/15: Before the main market opened, the FTSE surged upwards by almost 20 points. When things had settled a bit, I opened a short from 6759, but it was slow coming down, so I closed with a small profit (£9) to await the opening of the main market. Although I expected the market to drop, I was unprepared for the speed at which it did so. It is always difficult to join a "moving train" and not knowing how far it would come down, I remained in cash. I thought there was a lull in the decrease at about 9 am, so I went long at 6675. I didn't time my exit very well at all and emerged with only £1 when there was a lot more available. The market seemed to have stabilised near 6660, so I went long again at 6666. By now it was nearing 11 am and the market variance had dropped, so I took my profits at a modest £13 gain, but I was thankful for that as at one time I was £18 down. So I am £23 up on the morning.

The multi-day trend has now switched clearly to negative, and I will look for a good price to go short. It's certainly a pity I closed my short from 6759! Otherwise, I would be sitting on a profit of over £170, but that is the price for a low risk strategy.

I didn't make a very good job in the afternoon either. There was a surge on the Dow which presumably led to the surge on the FTSE. I did eventually go long, at 6719, just before 3 pm, but stupidly, I closed when things were looking a bit grim. I should have just suffered a bit longer and I ended up losing the £23 that I gained in the morning.

11/8/15: The FTSE was down this morning, but, unfortunately, I didn't take much advantage. I have noticed, however, that the China 300 index offered by IG can be quite volatile in a predictable way. The market seems to follow the same TA rules as the more established markets. So, as a trial, I made a trade and picked up £15. There was a lot more on the table but the swings were quite wild. I returned to the FTSE and went long after the fall, but it seemed to go into reverse and I chickened out closing with a £3 loss. I should have stayed the course and I would have picked up a good £10. When the main market opened it started dropping again, so I went short from 6705, closing at 6700 for a modest profit. I really do need to keep my positions running longer, but recent losses have undermined my confidence. Profit for the morning so far is £22.50, near enough the same as yesterday.

I made another trade in the morning going short at 6681, but the market then started turning around, so I closed for a small gain (£4). For much of the afternoon, the FTSE oscillated between about 6670 and 6690, but I didn't have the confidence to follow the admittedly small oscillations. When I did finally go long, near the end of the day, the market again moved against me, but I emerged with a tiny profit (£2). Still, all the little profits add up, so I am ahead £28 on the day.

12/8/15: At 6.30 am or so, I could see that the China 300 index was heading down, so I opened a short from 3867, closing just a few minutes later with a £21 profit. If I could have stomached the ride, there was another £100 there. Meanwhile, the drop in the Japanese (or the Chinese) market had triggered an overnight drop in the FTSE. Once the main market opened, the downward trend resumed, and I went short at 6606. But what was I thinking? I let the price oscillations worry me, and instead of riding the market down for a potential profit of over £100, I closed for a mere £4 profit, for a total of £25 for the morning so far. Not letting my positions run is really costing me a lot of potential profits.

For much of the morning, the FTSE started recovering, albeit with lower variance. Thinking that a further move up was in the offing, I foolishly went long just before midday at 6595. The paper losses continued to pile up and at one stage the position was almost £50 down. Fortunately, it recovered somewhat and I was able to close with just a small loss of £9. Again, thinking that the market was simply moving through a stable range, I went long again at 6581. This time, I didn't waste much time in closing my position and the loss on the trade was £21, completely wiping out my day's profit. Looking for some sort positive end to the day, I spotted the US 500 on the way up, and went long, picking up £8.50 for a quick trade. That meant that I ended the day a pound up!

13/8/15: The morning did not go very well. Following the pattern of recent days, before 7 am I traded the China 300 index, going short at 3822. It was a roller coaster ride, and at one point I was £90 down, in just a few minutes. In the end, I was happy to escape with a £12 profit. Overnight the FTSE had increased substantially, and once the main market opened, the initial direction was unclear. Thinking that the market had resumed its positive direction, I went long at 6634. That was a terrible move, as it was clear that I had bought on a spike. The market dropped substantially, and I panicked closing with a £48 loss. I should have closed my eyes and waited, as the market turned around again. Later in the morning, I spotted an opportunity to go short at 6617, and I picked up £11, but this took a while as the market variance had dropped. I am now £24 down on the morning.

I made only one more trade during the rest of the day. Having watched the market drop from about 1.30 pm onwards, I finally went short just after 3 pm only to find the market reverse. I escaped with a profit of £6 for a loss of £18 on the day.

14/8/15: Today was an uneventful day on the markets. I looked at the China 300 index early in the morning, and should have gone long just after 7 am, but I stayed on the sidelines. The FTSE didn't move much, but on two occasions I saw a buying opportunity. My entry prices were good (6562 at about 11.30 am and 6550 at about 2.30pm), but I didn't time my exits very well, and picked up only £4 in total.

We are now half way through August, and my profit for the month is just £27, a lot less than the £570 for July.

17/8/15: I made my customary foray into the China market, and just before 7 am opened a long position on the China 300 index at 3752.3. Initially, it went backwards, but soon after 7 am there was a surge and I closed at 3764.8 for a handy profit of £67.50. The FTSE opened with a downward trend, although it was difficult to pick out from the usual morning noise. Soon after 8 am, I opened a short at 6580. The position went backwards at first but then turned around and I closed at 6563 for a chunky £34 profit. The FTSE rose back up soon afterwards but has since dropped again. Total profit for the day so far is £101.

The FTSE drifted downwards for much of the afternoon, and by about 3 pm it looked to have stabilised. It started moving up, and I kept looking at it, but finally went long just as it breached the upper Bollinger band near 6540. I closed with a profit of £17, close to the maximum for that particular time. After retracing its steps, the market went through another wave, but I was content to stay on the sidelines with a profit of £119 for the day. Nice!

18/8/15: This morning I paid the price for trading a volatile market. After watching the China market for 10 minutes or so, I went long at 3638 at £5 per point. The timing was bad and the market crashed. I was confused by the technical analysis and expected a recovery at some point but that never came before my position collapsed. I closed with a loss of £315. I think perhaps I ought to stop trading the Chinese market unless the minimum per point is lower. £2 per point would make losses more forgiving.

In view of this morning's disaster, I didn't even look at the FTSE today, but instead did other things while contemplating my big loss, the largest in the almost 6 months that I have been trading actively. Looking again at my trade, I was too optimistic in thinking that the market had bottomed out. The trend over a couple of hours was down, and I should have been more cautious in going long. 50% of the time I would have been right and if it had been the FTSE, I could have got out with a loss of £50 or less. I have noticed before that the China index is volatile, which is its attraction to some extent, and it is therefore necessary to set wider mental stops than normally used for the FTSE. I did have the chance to escape with a loss of £80 at one point, but I was still thinking erroneously that the position would turn around. It didn't turn around and I might have closed earlier. Previously, I picked up modest gains for high risk, so today's trade was probably an accident waiting to happen. What is done is done, and at least if I had held on for dear life then by now I would be heavily at a loss, £900 down. So at least I substantially limited my loss. However, it does seem at the moment that I am not ready for the rapid movements in the China market - down 3.8% in 15 minutes(!), and I got out at a 2% loss on the market. It perhaps also suggests that I am making the standard mistakes of letting my losses run and cutting my wins early instead of the converse. I need to redouble my efforts to trade more logically to reduce the impact of trades like today. I hope that this lesson has been well learnt.

19/8/15: Today begins the long path to recover the losses of the month. I watched the China 300 index, but didn't trade. Overnight the FTSE had dropped but had stabilised near 6510 once the main market opened. The market fall was then re-established, and I went short at 6498. Mindful of yesterday's performance, I was happy to close at 6485 for a reasonable profit of £26 in less than 10 min. As usual, I should have held on another 30 min.

I made one more trade on the FTSE during the day, going long at 6452 in mid-afternoon, when I thought the market had stabilised. I closed at 6458, near the peak soon afterwards, for a profit of £12.60. Later the market plunged, and in hindsight I could have made a lot more money going short.

20/8/15: I was somewhat surprised by the reduction in the FTSE before the market opening, and after it appeared to have stabilised, I went long at 6368. At one point, the position was £8 up, but it then reversed, and I bailed out with a loss of £14.60. That turned out to be a mistake, as half an hour later, the market went upwards. It seemed a clear change of direction at the time, so I went long again, this time at 6380. The position went £18 into the black only for it to reverse just as quickly, and I closed with another loss of £9. If proof were ever needed, it is not easy to know when to close positions.

21/8/15: I have been a bit preoccupied the last day or so, so I wasn't able to take any advantage of yesterday's market crashes. Of course if I had been paying attention, I may have lost money. I started watching the FTSE100 again this morning and went long at 6301, but having lost confidence with my Chinese foray this week, I became a bit too concerned and closed at 6322. It was a nice £22 profit, but it could have been a lot more.

The FTSE drifted downwards for much of the afternoon, but it wasn't really clear whether this decrease was likely to continue, so I didn't make any trades. Instead I focused on the S&P 500, which generally moved downwards from the market opening at 2.30 pm. Occasionally, the S&P paused and I was able to go long, picking up some modest profits in 3 trades (£23.50, £13.50 and £11.00). None of these were optimal by any means, and I almost came a cropper on the last trade. Nonetheless, three trades like this combined with the FTSE trade netted a respectable £70 for the day. Perhaps this is a better strategy than my previous one: make an early trade on the FTSE and then switch to the S&P once the American market opens.

24/8/15: All the major stock indices crashed over the weekend. At one point the FTSE went below 6000, so there were opportunities to go long. By this morning, I spotted a couple opportunities and went long just before 7 am at 6015, but the market became very volatile and I closed for a loss of £27, thinking that the market was about to go back down again. The market did indeed drop but if I could have endured the temporary loss, I could have come out well ahead. The same thing happened an hour or so later: once the main market opened it started going up, so I went long from 6027. This time it went down significantly, so I closed with a loss of £59. That was also a mistake as the market turned around again and went over 6060. What a terrible start to the week!

25/8/15: There has been continual turmoil on the markets over the last 24 hours due to the financial situation in China. I was busy elsewhere, so I wasn't able to take advantage, or lose money! I looked at the markets from time to time, but I was too paralysed to make any serous trades. This morning, my paralysis continued as I saw the FTSE first drop below 5900 and then claw back most of the losses. By the time the main market opened I finally decided to take a long position, but it was all too late. For once I entered late at 5983 and closed late picking up just £17.40. At about 8.30 am I went long again at 5996.3, closing at 6007.8 for a profit of £40 for the morning so far. For someone mentally sharper than me, with a firmer constitution, there is a lot of money to be made (or lost) in this rapidly moving market.

I made one more trade on the FTSE, going long in late morning at 6057, having been watching it while too paralysed to act. The timing was terrible, and the FTSE went down significantly soon afterwards. I left it too late to close and lost £62, only to see the FTSE rise to over 6100 just before noon. By then I was out of the house anyway..... Once the American market opened I saw several opportunities on the S&P 500 in the afternoon and I began the business of clawing back my losses. Trading at £10 per pt (the IG minimum), I went long twice and short at about 4.45 pm, picking up £31, £16 and £16 quite painlessly. Perhaps I should stick to the S&P. Profit for the day was £41.

26/8/15: The market turmoil continued. Inadvisably, I made 3 trades on the S&P 500, but despite wide stops, I lost each trade, losing almost £250 on the day. Most of my July's profit has now been lost, primarily due to today's trades and my trades last week on the China market. I need to take steps to reduce risk. The S&P 500 is a very good market, if you can get it right, but wide swings such as have occurred recently, can be a problem.

In the evening, the FTSE appeared to have bottomed out, so I went long at 5962. In the space of about half an hour, the FTSE went up over 30 points, and I closed near the top for a profit of £61.60. I should have gone long again after the dip in the price, but I wasn't watching! The evening trade cut my loss for the day to £182, but low risk trading will be needed for the foreseeable future.

27/8/15: After the overnight rise, the FTSE had apparently settled and was starting to move down. I went short at 6077, just after 7 am, but further FTSE reductions didn't occur. I pulled out with a gain of just £1, and soon after the market rose significantly. Another shorting chance occurred just after 8 am when the main market opened. I opened at 6111 closing at 6100 for a gain of £21.40. The market dropped further but has since risen. For the moment it looks as if the market has settled near 6110 but it is still very variable so I'll refrain from further trades for the moment.

I made one more trade in the afternoon, going long at 6165, but the FTSE went down soon afterwards, and fearing for my life, I closed the position at a loss. This turned out to be premature, and I ended up just £1.80 up on the day.

28/8/15: I lost more money in the morning session on the FTSE, going long at 6220. The market was quite noisy and I ended up losing £17. I made another trade in late morning going short at 6199, but I should have held on and I could have got a decent profit. I have had too many losses recently and became too nervous, closing for a trivial profit. The same thing happened in the afternoon: my trades were too tentative, but I made enough to break even on the day. Next week is a fresh start, and hopefully I will be in a better frame of mind to trade more confidently.

31/8/15: Today being a UK holiday, the market was closed although the FTSE could be traded on IG. However, rather than pay the large FTSE spread, I decided to trade just the S&P 500. Unfortunately, I didn't make a very good job of it, taking out a long position in mid-morning which I closed for a loss of £27. The market recovered later, but not before dropping a few more points. When the main US market opened at 2.30 pm UK time, I opened a short at the right time, but the market movements were extreme and in a few seconds, my position went from a £20 gain to half that. I closed, only to find the profit reduced still further to just £1.

In the mid-afternoon I made another trade going long at 1974 but the volatility was too much for me to stomach and I closed for another £26 loss.

This brings to a close my trading for August, which ended with a significant loss of £360. It has wiped out most of the profit of £570 that I obtained in July. I hope now to draw a line under my recent more adventurous trades and keep it safe and simple starting tomorrow.

8. Summary and Conclusions

Trading the stock market via spread betting is certainly a potentially lucrative way of making money, but it is not easy. The average spread betting account lasts about 6 months before the holder gives up, presumably because he (and it's usually a he) loses too much money. Nonetheless with diligence and hard work, ones normal human failings can be curtailed to provide at least some income. The advantage of spread betting over other methods of investing is that once you have demonstrated for yourself that you can make money, all you need do is increase your risk level (i.e. the amount per point) and have higher potential profits. This requires a certain rigour in analysing your trades to make sure that your performance is not simply a matter of luck. However, no matter how confident you are that your trades will be successful in the long run, you may simply not be comfortable with taking a risk beyond a certain point, and this will tend to limit potential profits.

If you trade the FTSE, with minimum bet size of £2 per point, with practice you can average £40 per day and the typical risk for each trade might be about £20. But you may well have some bad days on which you might lose £100. On those days, the chances are that you will have broken all the rules. If you can keep to established principles, such losses should be rare. To get to the point where you are applying your own rules consistently may well take a few years, but learning the basics so that you are at least at break even need only take a few months.

Investing by Spread Betting, by John Austin

Ultimately, it is up to you to establish your own set of rules. I discussed this somewhat tongue in cheek in Chapter 5, in which I suggested that you have a mantra based on sound principles. In addition of course you should make extensive use of technical analysis (TA), which I described in brief in Chapter 3. Technical analysis works because human behaviour is essentially predictable and unchanging. It even seems to transgress race. For example, the same TA principles seem to apply to the Chinese, American, UK and European markets. Just because you know the theory, though, doesn't make it easy to apply. For example, I consistently close my positions too early according to the TA, but I seem powerless at times to do anything about it! Overall, then, you should take steps to avoid losing money. You may be betting with money that you "can afford to lose", as the spread betting companies like to say, but don't use this as an excuse for overly speculative forays into unknown territory! Your mantra then should contain guidelines as to how you will be limiting risk. These should include ideas such as using technical analysis, monitoring your positions carefully, don't bet against the market, limit your risk with an explicit or mental stop loss, keep plenty of equity in your account at all times etc. Also, get to know a chosen market and concentrate on that. All the same it is worth an occasional trade on a different market. Perhaps that will be more productive than the one you're used to. For example, I used to trade Forex, but switched to trading major indices (FTSE, S&P 500) once I saw how the TA principles worked. Of course professionals get to be able to trade several markets at once, but this is probably not for mortals like us!

This book concentrates on spread betting, but you may find options trading more to your taste. The financial risk is certainly less, but you pay heavily for it in increased market spreads and lower returns. It is not for me. Another thing to consider is automatic trading systems, discussed in Chapter 3. I have not used these in recent years. The idea is to write a computer program containing all the TA rules and get it to spit out a future trading recommendation. I'm sure that they can be very effective for some people, and of course they come at a price: typically you subscribe to a service. However, the puzzling thing about such systems, is if they are so good, why is everybody not using them? I have discussed some reasons why automatic systems may not work. Perhaps the most important idea is that the characteristics of the market are forever changing. One month it may be the Greek crisis, the next it may be a surge on the Tokyo or the US markets which drives global markets. This means that at different times, different trading models will give the best returns. In principle, as a person, you can respond to the changing market conditions. But it obviously takes time and effort to get to the point where you can understand a market and trade successfully.

Account progress since 1 April 2015. The dotted line is a linear regression line through the daily data, but this exaggerates the rate of growth of profit, as the last few weeks of the record have been disappointing. A more conservative approach, based on application of a lower risk strategy should pay dividends in the future.

This book forms Part 1, with Part 2 to follow in about 6 months' time. This book is largely based on my own experiences. I have learnt the basics and have established a set of rules that I try

Investing by Spread Betting, by John Austin

to follow. However, I know that I continue to make mistakes: I get too emotionally involved, I tend to open and close trades too early. Despite this, I have managed to make a small profit during this learning period. In future, I am planning to apply the learning and see whether I can extend my profits. I have chosen markets that are optimal for my risk profile (FTSE 100 and S&P 500). I will try to minimise the emotional element. I will try to close my losing positions quickly. I will try to run longer with my gains. I will trade at more optimum times of day. Check my website for up to date progress!

Acknowledgements

I would like to thank Anton Vella (People Plus) for his advice and encouragement during this project and for suggesting the writing of this book. Independently, my brother in law, David Ellery, also suggested writing this book, although I thought he had had too much red wine at the time! Although somewhat nervous at first about exposing my trading mistakes, I would also like to thank Anton for suggesting the publication of my financial blog on my website[34], which can be checked for my latest trades.

The print book version of this document was prepared with OpenOffice software, converted to pdf format and supplied to CompletelyNovel.com and Createspace.com for the production of print on demand copies. The electronic version of this book was prepared using Sigil.

Investing by Spread Betting, by John Austin

References

[1] The spread-betting attrition rate, The Motley Fool, Published in Investing on16 May 2012, http://news.fool.co.uk/news/investing/2012/05/16/the-spread-betting-attrition-rate.aspx, accessed 2 September 2015.

[2] Compare financial spread betting companies, Money, http://www.money.co.uk/financial-spread-betting.htm, accessed 2 September 2015.

[3] Trading and Taxes: is Spread Betting really Tax Free?, Trading Spread Betting, http://www.tradingspreadbetting.com/trade/trading-and-taxes, accessed 2 September 2015.

[4] The stop-loss order – make sure you use it, Investopedia, http://www.investopedia.com/articles/stocks/09/use-stop-loss.asp, accessed 2 September 2015.

[5] The mathematics of investing, http://www.field-theory.org/articles/markets/, accessed 2 September 2015.

[6] The pros and cons of automated trading systems, Investpedia, http://www.investopedia.com/articles/trading/11/automated-trading-systems.asp, accessed 2 September 2015.

[7] Technical analysis: Chart Patterns, Investopedia, 2015, www.investopedia.com/university/technical/techanalysis8.asp, accessed 2 September 2015.

[8] Double top and double bottom, Wikipedia, 19 July 2015, https://en.wikipedia.org/wiki/Double_top_and_double_bottom, accessed 2 September 2015.

[9] Head and shoulders (chart pattern), Wikipedia, 19 July 2015, https://en.wikipedia.org/wiki/Head_and_shoulders_(chart_pattern), accessed 2 September 2015.

[10] Cup and Handle, wikipedia, 28 June 2015, https://en.wikipedia.org/wiki/Cup_and_handle, accessed 2 September 2015.

[11] MACD, Wikipedia, 23 March 2015, https://en.wikipedia.org/wiki/MACD, accessed 2 September 2015.

[12] Moving average, Wikipedia, 23 August 2015, https://en.wikipedia.org/wiki/Moving_average, accessed 2 September 2015.

[13] Spread betting for losers: Part 1: How to break even, Enigmascientific.com, Science ebooks and print books, 31 August 2015,

Investing by Spread Betting, by John Austin

http://www.enigmascientific.com/ebooks/spreadbetting.html, accessed 2 September 2015.

[14] Bollinger bands, Wikipedia, 19 May 2015, https://en.wikipedia.org/wiki/Bollinger_Bands, accessed 2 September 2015.

[15] Relative strength index, Wikipedia, 27 August 2015, https://en.wikipedia.org/wiki/Relative_strength_index, accessed 2 September 2015.

[16] Straight To Hell, John Lefevre, Published by Grove Press, 16 July 2015.

[17] Trade with your brain, not your heart, Investorplace 247 trader, John Lansing, 13 November 2012, http://investorplace.com/247trader/trade-with-your-brain-not-your-heart/#.VdHhLvlViko, accessed 2 September 2015.

[18] Wait for the Confirmation of the trade, Stock trading strategies, Swing-Traders.eu, http://www.swing-traders.eu/stock-trading-strategies/4-wait-confirmation-trade, accessed 2 September 2015.

[19] The art of cutting your losses, Ken Hawkins, Investopedia, http://www.investopedia.com/articles/stocks/08/capital-losses.asp, accessed 2 September 2015.

[20] Let your profit run, Investopedia, http://www.investopedia.com/terms/l/letyourprofitrun.asp, accessed 2 September 2015.

[21] Why pros don't chase trades, Mark Soberman, Trader Kingdom, http://traderkingdom.com/trading-futures-education-topics/trading-psychology-trading-education/6670-why-pros-dont-chase-trades, accessed 2 September 2015.

[22] Trading against the trend, Jim Wycoff, Traders Log, http://www.traderslog.com/trading-against-trend/, accessed 2 September 2015.

[23] The guilt of trading too much, Jeff sommer, NY Times, 4 June, 2011, http://www.nytimes.com/2011/06/05/your-money/05stra.html?_r=0, accessed 2 September 2015.

[24] Time in the market, not market timing, Mitchell Tuchman, Forbes, 8 June 2015, http://www.forbes.com/sites/mitchelltuchman/2015/06/08/time-in-the-market-not-market-timing/, accessed 2 September 2015.

[25] Black Monday, Investopedia, http://www.investopedia.com/terms/b/blackmonday.asp, accessed 2 September 2015.

Investing by Spread Betting, by John Austin

[26] How to make and lose $2,000,000 day trading: the system and the story, http://startupbros.com/make-lose-2000000-day-trading-system-story/, accessed 2 September 2015.

[27] 5 traits that traders share with elite athletes, 16 December 2011, Babypips.com, http://www.babypips.com/blogs/pipsychology/5-traits-that-successful-traders-share-with-elite-athletes.html, accessed 2 September 2015.

[28] The financial markets: when fear and greed take over, Investopedia, http://www.investopedia.com/articles/01/030701.asp, accessed 2 September 2015.

[29] Fear of missing out, Wikipedia, 31 August 2015, https://en.wikipedia.org/wiki/Fear_of_missing_out, accessed 2 September 2015.

[30] 25 Inspirational quotes about money, Henrik Edberg, The Positivity Blog, http://www.positivityblog.com/index.php/2007/06/06/25-inspirational-quotes-on-wealth-and-money/, accessed 2 September 2015.

[31] Options basics tutorial, Investopedia, www.investopedia.com/university/options/, accessed 2 September 2015.

[32] Black-Scholes model, Wikipedia, 19 July 2015, https://en.wikipedia.org/wiki/Black%E2%80%93Scholes_model, accessed 2 September 2015.

[33] Efficient market hypothesis, Wikipedia, 27 August 2015, https://en.wikipedia.org/wiki/Efficient-market_hypothesis, accessed 2 September 2015.

[34] Finance blog: Is there any science in financial trading?, Enigmascientific.com, http://www.enigmascientific.com/finance, accessed 2 September 2015.

Investing by Spread Betting, by John Austin

John pictured at Bryce National Park, Utah, USA

About the Author

The Author, Dr. John Austin, has over 30 years' research experience on the upper atmosphere and has published over 80 papers in numerous international scientific journals. In addition John worked for 4 years as an Editor of the Journal of Geophysical Research, the premier Geophysics journal in the USA.

He has spent several years working in the USA, at NASA Langley, Hampton, virginia (1984-1985) and the University of Washington (1988-1990), where amongst other things he met his future wife Alda, to whom he is still married. During 2003-2011 John worked in Princeton, NJ, USA. His main scientific contribution has been to show the connection between ozone depletion and climate change. John has been involved in the writing of numerous international reports for the World Meteorological Organisation and The Intergovernmental Panel on Climate Change, for which the

Investing by Spread Betting, by John Austin
IPCC received the 2007 Nobel peace prize.

In recent years, John has broadened his work into popular science, through the website DecodedScience.com and in 2014 he created an internet scientific publishing business Enigma Scientific Publishing, http://www.enigmascientific.com. "Measuring the World" was his first popular science book. This book, "Spread Betting for Losers", applies his scientific experience to a subject close to most of our hearts!

****

When not working, John enjoys a variety of activities including chess, running, photography and travel. He also spends an unhealthy amount of time on mathematical puzzles and enjoying red wine!

22871392R00069

Printed in Great Britain
by Amazon